Architect?

The MIT Press
Cambridge, Massachusetts
London, England

Architect?

A Candid Guide to the Profession

Revised edition

Roger K. Lewis

This book was set in Palatino and Helvetica by The MIT Press.
Printed and bound in the United States of America.

Library of Congress Cataloging-in-Publication Data

Lewis, Roger K.
    Architect? : a candid guide to the profession / Roger K. Lewis. — Rev. ed.
       p.   cm.
    Includes bibliographical references and index.
    ISBN 0-262-12208-1 (alk. paper)
    1. Architecture—Vocational guidance—United States.   I. Title.
NA1995.L45   1998
720′.23′73—dc21   97–35747
                                                                                       CIP

For all the architecture students who I hope learned something from me and from whom I unquestionably learned a lot; and for my colleagues, friends, and family.

Contents

III Being an Architect

When I wrote the first edition of this book about the profession of architecture, my goal was to explain the true nature of architectural education and practice. I wanted to tell beginning architecture students and prospective architects, lucidly and honestly, what to expect. At the time, such a book seemed to be missing in the literature of architecture.

Since then, my goals for the book have not changed, but the culture and circumstances of architecture have. The profession is more diverse, as are architectural schools and degree programs. The use of computers has increased exponentially. New architectural philosophies, theories, and fields of exploration have appeared. And equally important, my own perceptions, interpretations, and judgments of architecture have evolved, along with my writing style (improved, I hope, by a dozen years of journalistic practice). In addition to an updated and enhanced text, I have added more illustrations to augment the book's storytelling effectiveness visually.

Despite revisions, *Architect?* remains faithful to its original intent: to offer a candid account of the realities of becoming and being an architect. A subjective work based substantially on my own experiences, observations, and analysis, it discloses the texture and complexity, the agonies and ecstacies, of being an architecture student and then a practicing architect. The book purposefully focuses on traditional architectural practice, since this is what most architects are educated for and what most prospective architects expect to do. Nevertheless, it also discusses other, related career options that graduate architects pursue in lieu of traditional practice.

Since finishing architectural school in 1967, I have taught and practiced architecture and advised, instructed, or employed hundreds of neophyte architects. But I have yet to encounter anyone who truly understood what he or she was getting into, either prior to embarking on an architectural career or, in many cases, after embarkation. Years of answering the question, What is it really like to be an architect? so often posed by students, clients, and others, have led me to tell and retell the story.

This book addresses anyone seriously contemplating becoming an architect: students in high school and college, those out of school thinking about reentering, beginning architecture students, and young architects just finishing school. Career guidance counselors and academic advisers should read or refer to this book before offering suggestions to their questing advisees. Architects' clients, or potential clients, should read it to learn the facts of life about the architects they hire, admire, or abuse. Finally, architects should read this book to see the extent to which it affirms or contradicts their own view of themselves and their personal experiences.

I assume that some readers seek basic information, while others look for basics plus elaboration and commentary. Thus I have tried to respond to both levels of interest, although readers may discover additional levels of intent and interpretation beyond these two. I especially hope that the illustrations complementing the text help illuminate or even validate the book's many contentions, which nevertheless represent solely my point of view.

The Contents reveals the specific topics treated but says little of the tone created by the author. For me, writing this book allowed an exploration of contrasts. The inside story of architectural education and practice is one of dualities: success and failure, acceptance and rejection, tedium and elation, fulfillment and disillusionment. The experiences of becoming and being an architect are bittersweet. Although my commentary about these experiences may not be shared by all, the issues raised are at least genuine and consequential. And anyone who has read this book will learn the unvarnished truth, like it or not.

Acknowledgments

I am indebted to many people. Too numerous to cite individually, they are friends, professional colleagues and acquaintances, clients, teachers, and students. Much expressed here comes from listening to them, although I take full responsibility for all that I say and advocate.

I have enjoyed the unqualified support of the University of Maryland School of Architecture and its three deans: John Hill, John Steffian, and Steven Hurtt. Several close friends, Samuel Gorovitz, Frank Schlesinger, Judith and Stanley Hallet, and John Hill, were especially helpful in providing advice and editorial suggestions for the first edition, started during a sabbatical leave in 1982. Another sabbatical leave in 1996–1997 made possible the writing of this revised edition, along with the continuing support of The MIT Press and its Acquisitions Editor, Roger Conover.

Since 1984, while teaching and practicing architecture, I have been writing "Shaping the City," a regular column on architecture and urbanism published by *The Washington Post.* This has provided me a unique opportunity to hone my journalistic and cartooning skills, for which I am very appreciative. Many of the illustrations in this revised edition of *Architect?* first appeared in "Shaping the City."

But the most important source of encouragement was my wife, Ellen, who for several years has urged me to update the book. I am especially grateful to her for both pushing me and for putting up with it all.

In 1960, during a severe sophomore year slump, I decided suddenly to switch my major from physics to architecture at the Massachusetts Institute of Technology. I was nineteen. At age seventeen I had entered MIT to become a scientist or engineer, but by the fourth semester of college, I faced the common dilemma of not knowing what to be or do. I only knew that I wanted to work in the tangible, three-dimensional world and that I would probably not find this in the arcane world of quantum physics.

I sought advice from family, friends, and teachers. Architecture was suggested because I had always enjoyed art and graphics, possessed drawing talent, and had demonstrated technical aptitude. I had never considered architecture before, since I knew

nothing about it. Brief visits to MIT's architecture department stimulated my interest, mostly because of student project drawings scattered about and pinned up on walls. In that stressful spring, architecture seemed to be the answer.

Following my decision, the little information and insight I actually had about architecture proved no obstacle to exciting speculation. I could foresee a wonderfully romantic, exalted profession promising intellectual rewards, wealth and prestige, an amalgam of art and technology fused together by social idealism and creative energy. As an architect I would be marshaling diverse resources and mastering many skills to create artfully designed and executed buildings, each a monument to its architect's genius. I would be a generalist and a specialist at the same time, a recognized professional, a purveyor of culture as well as a provider of services to a needy clientele.

Heroic names like Frank Lloyd Wright and Le Corbusier, accompanied by visions of skyscrapers and beautiful drawings, came to mind. A heady realm of aesthetics, construction, appreciative clients, a respectful public, and the newly awakened 1960s social consciousness beckoned. It appeared that architects were in the middle of it all, orchestrating a kind of real-world opera.

In retrospect, there is nothing unusual about the way I and others make our decisions to become architects. People choose careers for many reasons, often knowing relatively little about their choice at the outset. Many careers appear inscrutable or mysterious to the uninitiated, the nature of which is discovered only after initiation. Although architecture is no exception, its real attributes differ greatly from those so often ascribed to it. Countless students, clients, and consumers of architecture possess incredibly meager, if not erroneous, knowledge or comprehension of how architects think and function. Indeed, most people's notions about accountants, bankers, pilots, doctors, truck drivers, attorneys, or plumbers better approximate reality than their notions about architects.

Few people ever require an architect's services. Most do not even know an architect. What they might know is the explosive Howard

Ruark, embodied on the silver screen by Gary Cooper in Ayn Rand's *The Fountainhead;* urbane, blue-eyed Paul Newman reading electrical diagrams in his office boudoir in the *Towering Inferno;* the daddy in television's *Brady Bunch;* or the vengeful vigilante, portrayed by Charles Bronson in the movie *Death Wish,* whose primary project activity consisted of shooting hoodlums in the streets and subways of New York City (he eventually branched out to Chicago). Architects as depicted in film and television can be heroes, lovers, fools, or miscreants. But I can think of no popular account about an architect's being an architect in the way that doctors are portrayed practicing medicine or attorneys are portrayed practicing law.

The account that follows is unlikely to become popularized, but it will tell aspiring architects reasons for being or not being an architect, what being an architect means, and how to become one.

I

To Be or Not to Be . . .
an Architect?

1

Why Be an Architect?

Deciding to become an architect should be a positive decision predicated on positive expectations. What can you expect? What are the rewards and motivations that lead men and women to invest five to eight years in rigorous university and professional education, three or more years in internship, and subsequent decades pursuing architectural practice, teaching, scholarship, or research?

Money and Lifestyle

Let us begin with an obvious incentive to which most people can relate: money. Most people pursue a career or profession to earn a living, among other things, and to enhance their potential incomes. But professionals' incomes can vary dramatically, especially in the field of architecture. Some architects earn only enough to ensure survival, while others achieve relative affluence. Each earning level supports corresponding lifestyle choices. Because architects are frequently associated with people and circumstances reflecting costly lifestyles, the public assumes that architects are affluent, well-to-do, big-income professionals. Some are. Most are not.

It is possible to achieve substantial wealth as an architect—and no doubt some architects pursue this as a primary personal goal—but it is improbable. Instead, most architects earn comfortable or modest livings, enjoying reasonable but limited economic stability and prosperity. Average incomes in the profession of architecture are solidly middle class, comparable to what school teachers, plumbers and electricians, sales representatives, and nurses earn.

Graduate architects begin their careers as wage earners drawing hourly, monthly, or annual salaries reflecting prevailing marketplace conditions. After three years of internship and further practice, they may become associates or principal owners of firms, either in partnership with others or as sole proprietors. Larger firms typically provide larger incomes at all levels, from senior partner down to newly employed draftsperson.

Architects who earn large incomes can live very well. Frequently they live in interesting houses modishly decorated and furnished. They may travel to exotic places, ski, own sailboats, or escape to vacation cottages in the mountains or by the sea. They may collect art, entertain extensively, make substantial political campaign contributions, or support charitable causes and institutions. All of this costs money, which most wage earners lack.

For the majority of less affluent architects, there are nevertheless ample lifestyle choices not so dependent on high incomes. Many architects find great satisfaction living modestly in cities, suburbs, small towns, or rural areas. Their lifestyles may be more basic, even approaching subsistence at times, but they also may enjoy flexibility and freedom of a kind not found chasing economic success, the cash flow treadmill requiring continuous movement and lubrication.

Some architects have discovered other means, outside traditional architectural practice, to sustain themselves financially. Perhaps the ideal way to practice architecture is not to be obliged to make a living at it. Thus, architects have become real estate developers or construction contractors, sometimes making (or losing) much more money than is possible just from design practice. Architects teach in architectural schools, where they can sometimes earn in nine months what they could earn in twelve in an office. Still others, either by good fortune or design, enhance or stabilize their family income through their spouses' assets or earnings. Of course, the easiest route is to inherit money, but few are so endowed. Those who are can practice architecture as an impassioned hobby.

At times, earning money can be a serious problem for architects, and as we shall see later, adequate and consistent compensation is an ongoing problem for the entire profession. Unlike some other businesses and professions, architecture is not a field to enter to become rich by today's standards. The odds are against it. But you can earn a decent living at it most of the time, even if you are not exceptionally talented—and if you do not mind a little belt tightening from time to time.

Social Status

Social status is another reason you might choose architecture as a career. An elusive notion at best, it implies the achievement of a certain elevated place in society's hierarchy of who people are and what they do. Social status is relative, meaningful only in comparison with other professions or vocations. Society assumes that architects are educated, and both artistically sensitive and technically knowledgeable. Society does not know exactly how architects operate, but it does know that they often create monumental designs for monumental clients. As a result architects may be well respected or admired by members of a social system who, unfortunately, think less of people they consider lacking in education, less talented, and less acceptable in the company of people of wealth, influence, or so-called breeding.

Pursuing social status for its own sake is a dubious undertaking. But we are all aware of status, and for many people high status may become a desirable and explicit goal. It is fulfilling and ego boosting to be respected, to be invited places and seen by people one admires, or to be praised by peers whose opinions one solicits. As professionals, architects generally associate with other professionals, people in the creative arts, or people in business or government. In many cultures architecture is among the most respected of all professions, and the United States is no exception. The American Institute of Architects has reported that millions of Americans—especially college graduates younger than age forty-five—have expressed an interest in architecture. And any architect will tell you that frequently he or she has heard people say that they should have or could have become architects.

As a corollary to social status, the possibility of becoming part of the so-called establishment may motivate some architects. Read "establishment" to mean the power structure within a community, town, or city, since architects rarely can become part of national power structures other than those created by and for academic and cultural elitists. Belonging to the establishment means having close connections to business, civic, and governmental interests, being seen as a force to be reckoned with among influential peers of the local realm.

Establishment status means having your name recognized by people you do not know, being asked to serve on boards and committees, being sought periodically by the press, being invited to fund-raising functions, and knowing what is going on behind the scenes—being an insider to the off-the-record deliberations that occur in all communities, large and small, and that invariably involve those who see themselves as the power elite. Clearly social and establishment status are closely linked.

Fame

Beyond achieving economic and social status is the lure of fame. Fame can come without wealth, and in architecture it often does. To become publicly recognized, if not celebrated, can be an end in itself above all others. Everyone can name at least one or two famous architects, and architects can name dozens. To be famous usually requires that an individual do something exceptional and that others see, judge, and, most important, report it to a receptive and interested audience, preferably on a national or worldwide scale. Exceptional deeds may be constructive or destructive, as long as they are exceptional and therefore noteworthy.

Most architects become famous in a gradual way by doing work that eventually is recognized for its excellence. Often such work is seen as innovative or avant-garde in its early stages, with subsequent stages being periods of refinement and variation. A few architects seek innovation with every project. In all cases, fame is established and measured by professional consensus, coupled with judgments made by historians, critics, and journalists. For example, consider the following item from the *Wall Street Journal* (May 26, 1982, p. 33): "Fifty-eight deans and heads of accredited schools of architecture recently listed this country's top architects of non-residential structures. The overwhelming winner was I. M. Pei, who was mentioned by nearly half of the deans. . . . Rounding out the top ten were Romaldo Giurgola, Cesar Pelli, Kevin Roche, Philip Johnson, Gunnar Birkerts, Michael Graves, Charles Moore, Edward Larrabee Barnes and Richard Meier."

All of these architects are well known to other architects, but few are well known to the public. Fifteen years previously, the list would have been quite different. Today, only a few of those names would be on such a list, and fifteen years from now, today's list will have changed again. And ultimately, what is the real meaning or validity of composing a list of ten top architects (imagine lists of the "top ten" lawyers, dentists, police chiefs, chemical engineers, dermatologists, or newspaper editors!)?

For architects, fame and recognition come through the publicizing and publishing of what they do, say, or write. This means not only designing and building projects but also winning awards for projects and having them appear in journals, magazines, or newspapers. It means boosting and being boosted. Lecturing and writing about one's work and philosophy, being talked and written about by others, winning or judging competitions: all boost fame and thrust architects into the professional limelight.

Today events unfold so quickly that acts of provocation and revolution promise fame more readily. There appears now to be more explicit striving for notoriety and celebrityhood as ends in themselves. Architects, perhaps more than other professionals, consciously or subconsciously harbor a desire for fame, since so much of their work is public. What we do shows, after all. Perhaps we are in a kind of show business. Being famous may have its problems, but it is a form of public certification—a validation of success and a salvation from anonymity. Who has not fantasized about making the cover of *Time* magazine? It is not easily attainable, but it is possible. For architects, fame usually produces a desirable side effect: more clients and commissions. Pursuing fame may be good business. Unfortunately, fame can be fleeting, done in by overexposure, rapidly changing fashions, and shifting tastes.

Immortality

Fame can be not only ephemeral but also ultimately insufficient. If we contemplate basic human drives, procreation and perpetuation come to mind. What better way to transcend one's biological life than through the creation of potentially ageless and permanent structures that, even as future ruins, might tell future archaeologists, historians, and cultural legatees the story of who we were and what we did. Most people settle for their succeeding offspring and family heirlooms to memorialize themselves, but architects can leave behind architecture as monuments to themselves.

It may seem presumptuous or self-aggrandizing, yet it also seems natural for creative individuals to desire to make something that could endure forever. I recall thinking about this explicitly when I was a student making comparisons between architecture and other careers. Only architecture seemed to provide the opportunity to create something lasting and immortal. The architect, I thought, survives and lives forever through his or her work. Even if my name was forgotten, I naively believed that my constructed offspring would not be.

Probably many architects share this rather romantic, immortality impulse, even if consciously denying or resisting it. Properly understood and channeled, it is a perfectly healthy impulse, not a conceit. A commendable work of architecture is in part a statement of and about its architect, the architect's progeny ultimately left behind. Of course, good architecture has many parents. Thus parenthood must be attributed not only to the architect but also to the client and those who build, and to the society and culture of which architecture is a part.

Contributing to Culture

Good architects see themselves as more than professionals who render services to fee-paying clients. Architecture is an expression and embodiment of culture and cultural conditions, or even a critique of culture. The history of architecture and the history of civilization are inseparable. Indeed, architectural historians spend their professional lives studying, analyzing and interpreting architecture not only to understand architecture, but also to understand the political, social and economic systems that produced it. By designing and building, architects know that they may be contributing directly to culture's inventory of ideas and artifacts, no matter how insignificant. Thus the search for appropriate cultural achievement is an important motivation for architects.

Think about the past, and bring to mind images of successive cultures and civilizations. One cannot help but see architecture in the mind's eye. Pyramids in Egypt, Greek and Roman temples, Gothic cathedrals, medieval castles and townscapes, Renaissance churches and squares, English houses and gardens, Asian pavilions, industrial-age cities and skyscrapers come into view. Architecture is an indispensable component of even the most unsophisticated cultures. If asked to describe the world of American Indians, what child would fail to sketch a teepee? Think of Neanderthals, and you will soon think of caves.

Unfortunately, not all architectural work offers opportunities for cultural enrichment. But when such opportunities do arise, however modest, the architect's contribution may be unprecedented, suggesting new directions in form and style, technology, or methods of design. Or the work may reaffirm or refine already established

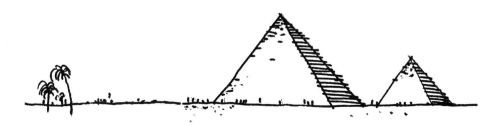

cultural norms and iconography. Rather than inventing something new, the architect may be adding to the growing collection of cultural works completed or in progress. Innovation and revolution require subsequent development and evolution. Architects must cover the field.

Helping and Teaching Others

Many architects are driven by humanitarian motives. The desire to help or teach other people can be very strong, and since architecture can both render public service and serve as public art, architects can easily fulfill this desire. Most architects view themselves as benefactors to society—as humanists and humanitarians. Even when designing commercial projects for profit-motivated clients, architects believe that they have an additional, equally important client: the public. They feel an obligation to all who may use, occupy, or see the buildings they design, in both the present and the future—an obligation not only to provide shelter and accommodate activities but also to instruct and inspire.

When buildings are finished and put into use, it is very fulfilling for the architect to know that the client, the users, and the public appreciate and benefit from his or her efforts. Sometimes architects create environments that truly affect the lives of people in positive ways, perhaps by improving their living standards, behavior, sense of well-being and security, or their attitudes. Studies have shown that building occupants can feel better physically and psychologically, work more effectively, and be more productive in artfully designed environments. Well-chosen proportions, good light and color, appealing textures and details, pleasant views, comfortable furniture, desirable acoustical qualities, adequate ventilation, and thermal comfort can have great impact on body and mind. What a tremendous reward it is for architects to hear clients or users express satisfaction and gratitude for the architect's successful intervention in their lives.

Public-spirited architects contribute in ways other than designing buildings. Being adept in matters of organization, coordination, and advocacy, some architects have been successful in assisting needy individuals, communities, and special-interest groups to develop projects, preserve buildings, or save neighborhoods. Although architects in these situations may not produce designs or drawings, their efforts and know-how may lead to worthwhile building or better environmental sensitivity. Like fame, yet in a very different manner, doing for others elevates our ego and validates our sense of achievement and self-worth.

Teaching is giving, and although it is not always financially rewarding, it offers architects opportunities for lasting nonmonetary enrichment. First, professing and conveying knowledge to others is inherently enjoyable and satisfying. Second, teaching provides teachers with as much intellectual stimulation and education as it provides students. Third, academic freedom and flexibility of schedule allow teachers of architecture to practice, write, travel, or conduct research, as well as teach. Thus motivated teachers provide an exchange function, taking in or developing new ideas and information and then passing them on to their students in turn. Such interaction can be profound and enduring. Perhaps a teacher's greatest reward is seeing former students successfully applying what they have learned or following in their mentors' footsteps. Nothing compares with hearing a student tell you that what you conveyed at some earlier time is still remembered, still relevant, and still appreciated.

The Rewards of Creativity and Intellectual Fulfillment

Much of what architects do is driven by the force of human intellect and rational thinking. But human emotions operate as well. For architects the marriage of intellect and emotion is manifest in the impulse to be creative—to think, feel, do, and make. Good architects are compelled by their own will and passion to be architects and by the intellectual and emotional gratification that creativity can provide.

The creative impulse is difficult to explain but easy to recognize. It appears early in life and is experienced to some extent by all human beings. To begin with nothing but raw materials and random thoughts, and then to transform them into something tangible, well crafted, and stimulating to the mind and senses, is the essence of creativity. For the architect, creating buildings offers countless moments of elation.

Creating something beautiful and aesthetically well composed—a work of art—is the primary goal of many architects. Their chief concern is to design artifacts—whether cities or buildings or pieces of furniture or teapots—to look at and admire as one would look at and admire paintings or sculpture. Even if others dislike the design, the architect's eye still beholds the beauty that he or she alone has bestowed on the world.

Creativity is not limited to generating works of art. The creative mind takes pleasure in making things that work, whether buildings, machines, or toys. A substantial part of practicing architecture consists of creating physical environments that perform successfully. In other words, in addition to being artistic expressions, buildings must creatively accommodate human functions, be buildable from many components and materials, provide shelter from the elements, resist the forces of nature while preserving natural resources, and be affordable. Meeting both performance and aesthetic objectives simultaneously is architecture's greatest creative challenge.

Once that challenge is taken up, the excitement of design is matched only by the excitement of realization. Seeing one's design actually constructed is elating both emotionally and intellectually, and the rewards of responding to creative impulses are intensified by the struggles that accompany creativity. As we shall see, overcoming adversity absorbs much of an architect's energy, since many obstacles stand in the path along which architects and their projects travel. Sometimes just getting a project built is a victory, and when it is good architecture, the victory is even sweeter.

Architecture must accomplish many things for many different people, and diverse skills are required of architects to deal with the complexities of the design and construction process. Thus some of the intellectual fulfillment of practicing architecture lies in mastering these diverse skills and applying them successfully to difficult problems. Creative, rational minds often take great pleasure in solving puzzles, analyzing complicated systems, organizing data, examining multiple options, and accomplishing specific tasks. Architecture provides fertile ground for such minds to plow.

Let us examine the array of intellectual opportunities suggested here. Architecture entails activities of both mind and body acting in concert—thinking, drawing, crafting, seeing. The architect must know not only how to draw a line but also why and when. The senses must all be engaged to observe so that the mind can analyze and synthesize. Ideas must be communicated and explained graphically and verbally. What then are the specific aptitudes or talents that contribute to mastering and enjoying the art and discipline of architecture?

Graphic and visual skills The ability to see and to express things in graphic form.

Technical aptitude Proficiency in mathematics and scientific analysis (not necessarily in a particular science).

Verbal skills The ability to read, write, and speak, to organize or analyze effective verbal expression.

Organizational skills The ability to analyze and synthesize, to create order and direction out of disorder and chaos.

Memory The ability to store and recall information, images, or ideas.

Compositional talent The artistic ability to compose aesthetically successful visual form in two and three dimensions.

These are all essential to being an architect; they are the prerequisites for intellectual and emotional fulfillment in architecture. They also reflect the multidisciplinary nature of the field—the need for architects to be artists, craftspersons, draftspersons, technologists, social scientists, managers, accountants, historians, theoreticians, philosophers, gamblers, and other things to boot. Mobilizing talents in an arena so rich and diverse can be

tremendously exhilarating and rewarding, as stimulating as any
other career could be.

Love of Drawing

Although the discussion of creativity and intellectual fulfillment
talks briefly of the rewards of graphic exploration and invention, a
further note about drawing itself seems appropriate. For many
architects, drawing is an extremely satisfying and stimulating use
of time and energy—an activity that is its own reward.

Drawing can be loved. It can be therapeutic, requiring great concentration and the masking out of all other distractions or preoccupations. It is personal, since no two people draw exactly alike. For
design, the most vital kind of drawing, and probably the most

enjoyable, is sketching (as opposed to drafting). Sketching is the most spontaneous, the most plastic, and the most interpretive kind of drawing. Through sketching, architects both record and analyze impressions and explore and express new ideas or visions. Drafting, whether by hand or computer, merely transforms sketched ideas into analogs of reality.

Drawing architectural forms—buildings, spaces in buildings, land-scapes, urban spaces, or furniture—must become as natural for an architect as writing or reading. In fact, many architects would probably prefer to sit and draw, if given the choice, than to do most of the other work that architectural practice demands. Often the romance with drawing is taken to extremes. Architects may produce drawings whose abstract graphic qualities outweigh those of the design represented by the drawings. Some designers and draftspersons spend more time crafting and rendering the draw-ings themselves than they spend developing and perfecting their architectural ideas. And we frequently see architects' drawings that are so seductive, so artfully composed and so evocative that we overlook the merits of the subject depicted by such drawings.

If you like drawing, and particularly freehand drawing, then you may grow to love it as an architect. If you do not like to draw, if you find it tedious or difficult, then architecture may not be the right choice. The passion for drawing, and the drawing techniques architects develop and master, are unique to this profession.

Fulfilling the Dictates of Personality

In considering reasons to be an architect, we cannot overlook attributes of personality and their role in shaping careers. These attributes may be disregarded or underestimated by students and career counselors, but they are of great importance in determin-ing career choices and directions. In the real world outside the classroom, personal characteristics—let us say personality—may have a greater influence on one's life than all of the intellectual skills, talents, and knowledge that one possesses. The rewards in architecture, like most other professions, depend as much on personal and behavioral traits as on IQ, college transcripts, or good intentions.

All personal attributes matter, but some matter more than others. A sampling follows:

Self-confidence and ego strength Believing that you are capable, able to compete, perform well, and succeed.

Ambition Wanting vigorously to accomplish and succeed.

Dedication and persistence Committing and sticking to a cause or task, with a willingness to work hard at it.

Resilience Coping well with setbacks, criticism, failure; being able to bounce back and overcome.

Amiability Being able to affiliate and get along with others (who may not be close friends), to collaborate and participate.

Empathy Recognizing, understanding, and identifying with the circumstances and feelings of others.

Charm and poise Behaving so others see you as well-mannered, witty, thoughtful, friendly, and comfortable to be with.

Leadership Being able to persuade and inspire others to follow you or embrace your proposals and to make decisions, however well informed or ignorant.

Courage Willingness to take risks others shun, to experiment, venture into new territory, lose as well as win.

Passion Capacity for intense feelings about activities, people, ideas, places, or things.

This inventory does not constitute a complete list of requirements for being an architect, nor is it unique to this profession. However, measured doses of all of these attributes seem to be present in many good architects. And the lack of some of these attributes can prove to be a serious liability to achieving architectural goals, or even to becoming an architectural school graduate. In a discipline where criticism and negative judgments abound, lacking confidence, resilience, and persistence can be personally devastating, notwithstanding any native talents.

By contrast, an architect of mediocre talent but blessed with great charisma (an amalgam of several attributes, especially leadership, self-confidence, and charm) may always do very well. Such charisma may have more impact on an architect's career than any measurable competencies learned in an educational program. The ability to sell and to guide other people may ultimately accomplish more for you than the ability to draw, calculate, operate a computer, or even think great thoughts.

Anyone contemplating architecture as a profession should take serious stock of his or her personality. With assorted combinations of individual traits and in appropriate intensities, architecture can be the ideal profession in which to capitalize on such traits. Indeed, some people seem to have been born to be architects; they possess a mixture of intellect, talent, skills, and personal qualities—some of which are unquestionably genetic in origin—that makes architecture their undeniable cup of tea.

Freedom to Do Your Own Thing

Perhaps because architects are thought of as creative and artistic, society accepts their periodic departures from conventional behavior and attitudes, or even expects it at times. Many architects do live up to their image, exhibiting idiosyncrasies in the ways they dress, talk, and work or in their beliefs. They strive to be individualistic and nonconformist, if not radical. Frank Lloyd Wright, wearing his reputed cape and haughty expression, defied and decried all, becoming a prototype for iconoclastic architects.

Thus for anyone so inclined, architecture may be more attractive as a career than, say, banking, accounting, or military service. There is a kind of ego satisfaction and feeling of exceptionality that stems from being unique and different, from standing out, getting noticed and being remembered.

Architects appear to have more options for doing their thing their way in our culture, especially in comparison to other learned professions. They seem to have more freedom to shape and control the image of themselves that they project to their peers, their clientele, and the public. This image is reinforced by the work they do, the architectural values they espouse, the people with whom they associate, the causes they support, and the style in which they live. Few other careers offer this range of choice in how to behave and practice. Almost anything goes in architecture if it is done with panache. For this reason, architecture may be the most liberal of the established professions, the most tolerant and encouraging of deviation.

Finally, there is yet another reason for being an architect. Many architects really know how to have a good time, to let go when necessary. Starting first as students indulging in absurdities in school, architects have always found imaginative ways to relieve the pressure and stridency of architectural work. The fun comes through being whimsical, creating visual anecdotes or puns, and designing fantasies, as well as through more conventional recreational means. But the good times and amusing diversions are needed for still another purpose. As the next chapter explains, architecture has its negative side, and having a good time can help architects cope with bad times.

2

Why Not to Be an Architect

It may seem heretical and treasonous to the profession of architecture to cite reasons not to be an architect, much less to devote a whole chapter to it. But the story would be both incomplete and misleading if it failed to include the less-than-wonderful aspects of being an architect. Whenever we are told why we should do something, there may be unstated reasons why we should not. This is reinforced by experience, sometimes painfully. Painting the entire picture of becoming and being an architect at least gives you the chance to make informed decisions, to accept or reject, without feeling that there has been misrepresentation

Reasons not to be an architect are a matter of judgment. Therefore what follows are my own observations and interpretations of commonly encountered risks, roadblocks, and sources of frustration. Some are typical of many trades or professions, and others are more unique and endemic to architecture. At one time or another, virtually every architect has been plagued by some or all of these problems, felt overwhelmed or disillusioned by them. Unfortunately, knowing about and anticipating them makes them no less obstructive.

The Odds of Making It

Anyone contemplating a career in architecture should know that statistically there may be less than a fifty-fifty chance of ultimately becoming a licensed architect. Many undergraduate students who select architecture as their major will never complete the professional program and receive an accredited degree in architecture. Architecture students drop out along the way for various reasons, such as changing interests, amount and difficulty of work required, or loss of motivation.

Moreover, not all of those graduating from schools with accredited professional degrees will become registered and practice architecture. Some will change fields for various reasons, usually related to their feelings about their prospects as architects. They may be attracted to other fields for economic reasons or because they have talents more suitable to other career options. Some women with architectural degrees suspend working to have families, finding it difficult to pursue their careers in architecture and raise children at the same time. Regrettably, some never return to architectural practice.

Although the rate of student attrition and dropping out is high, there is no shortage of architects in the United States, especially in metropolitan areas, where most projects are built. Many architects, and some educators, believe that there are in fact too many architects and too many architectural firms. In addition, surveys of firms conducted by the American Institute of Architects (AIA) show that approximately one-fourth to one-third of architects in firms are owners or principals (proprietors, partners, or corporate officers). In other words, the majority of working architects are employees, not employers.

These statistics suggest a low probability that someone setting out to be a practicing architect will end up being an architect, and an even lower probability that they will actually become an owner or principal of a firm. Such statistical chances are not very encouraging. Yet we know that attrition and unrealized goals are normal in any academic undertaking or career; people change their minds and majors with ease and regularity. Nevertheless, attrition in architecture is unusually pronounced, and those who make it through and enter practice, despite the odds, still face tough challenges.

Lack of Work

Of all the difficulties architects face, periodic lack of work is proba-bly the most frustrating. The inability of individuals to find employment, or of firms to obtain commissions, is a major cause of economic and psychological suffering for practicing architects.

Employment for firms and individuals is directly related to both local and national economic conditions. When times are good and economic growth occurs, income, savings, and investment increase. Investing in building increases, which means architects get busier. Correspondingly, lack of economic growth, recession, inflation, and high interest rates diminish incomes, savings, and investment, especially in real estate. Building activity diminishes as well, along with the number of architectural commissions. Therefore the overall amount of work for architects is determined by the volatile and unpredictable conditions of the economy, over which architects have no control. Architects must constantly face the possibility of being under- or unemployed from one year to another.

Lack of work can also result from more localized conditions that the architect is unable to influence. Even if the general economy is strong, municipal or state economic circumstances may be unsta-ble or in decline. Since architects work on a project-by-project basis, their employment fate is intimately linked to the fate of each client and project. Architects are hired by clients when projects are conceived and laid off when projects are suspended or terminated.

Projects are financed by lending institutions or government agen-cies, built by contractors, and bought, leased, or used by the pub-lic. Thus the building process is complex, and for many reasons projects can start and stop abruptly. Because so much time and money can be invested in the architect's work on any single project, even the loss of one or two projects can be economically disastrous to a firm. Were architects rendering services to hun-dreds or thousands of clients at a time, this risk would be greatly reduced. But with most offices working on only a few projects over many months or years, the risk of not having work is increased.

Sometimes work can fall off dramatically. For example, in 1974 the economic expansion that had continued steadily for almost three decades, with only minor abbreviated recessions, abruptly ended. Architects were laid off at a rate not seen since the depression era of the 1930s. In my own office I was forced to let go most of my professional staff—a dozen architects—when work suddenly stopped in late 1973 and 1974. It was an agonizing act of retrenchment. Some firms became mere shadows of their former selves, shrinking by 70 or 80 percent.

In Cambridge, Massachusetts, on a day referred to as "black Friday," one of the country's largest and most prestigious architectural firms laid off close to one hundred employees because projects underway stopped abruptly. Fortunately this is not a typical, everyday occurrence. And young architects tend to be mobile, moving from firm to firm with rising and falling work loads, as well as for personal reasons. Employment follows projects, an inescapable fact of architectural life.

Competition

The threat of having no work is made worse by another ever-present factor: intense competition. As if economic uncertainty were not enough, there is the problem of too many architects chasing too few jobs. Competition in the field of architecture is keen and unending. It begins in school, carries over into the beginning years of job seeking and employment, and continues in the marketplace of practice.

Competition is certainly not unique to architecture, being integral to any free enterprise system, but in architecture it can reach astounding proportions. For example, in the period following the 1973–1974 oil embargo and recession, it was not uncommon to see as many as one hundred firms competing for a single, small, government project pursuant to an agency's announcing that it was looking for architects. When times are tough, architects can spend months looking unsuccessfully for jobs, because the number of competitors is so great in comparison to the amount of available work. In such periods architects may be forced to survive on unemployment benefits.

The intensity of competition results not only from an apparent oversupply of architects but also from the methods by which architects compete with one another. Architects are challenged by their colleagues in two ways: by their sheer numbers and by their ability and willingness in many cases to mount effective, aggressive campaigns to woo clients. Competing successfully today requires both soft and hard selling—the tactics of marketing and public relations, which may prove distasteful to some architects.

Inadequate Compensation

It is possible, but unlikely, for architects to earn hefty incomes—the kinds of incomes earned by doctors, lawyers, professional athletes, corporate executives, and Wall Street brokers. Indeed, no one should go into architecture to make a lot of money. Be an architect for many other reasons but not to get rich.

Given the numbers of architects and the competition, financial remuneration accompanying architectural employment may not be the greatest. Typically most architects believe that they are not adequately compensated and certainly not well compensated for what they do. When the American Institute of Architects asked registered architects if they "feel that in comparison to other professions, architects receive adequate fees for services they provide?" 85.7 percent said no. When asked if they "feel that employers compensate their architect employees adequately?" 67 percent answered no. Architects can earn enough most of the time to live comfortably, but few will ever match income and assets with their contemporaries who practice medicine, law, or accounting or who own successful businesses. Architects may have more fun, but they will probably have less money.

For many architectural firm owners, annual income can fluctuate widely. Good years can be followed by bad years—years in which a principal's income could be at the poverty level or could be negative (a loss). Architects' dependency on economic and project circumstances differentiates their income pattern from that of most other professionals whose earnings consistently increase over time and who stay busy whether times are good or bad. Moreover the majority of architects do not earn incomes significantly greater than the national median, which is not the case for established professionals in many other fields.

The compensation problem is not new. Decades ago, during an especially inflationary period in the United States, the problem was highlighted by an AIA survey, *Architects Compensation in Perspective*:

> Nominal total compensation has increased over the period 1970-81 by 59 percent for principals, 80 percent for supervisors, 66 percent for Technical I staff, 57 percent for Technical II staff and 70 percent for Technical III staff. . . . Inflation measured by the Consumer Price Index (CPI) has risen 140 percent since 1970. . . . It is apparent that real income for principals and all other staff in architecture firms has declined both nationally and regionally.

> . . . Comparing the increases in principals' compensation with increases in construction wages and salaries and compensation for miscellaneous professional services for the 1970–81 period . . . again, compensation for architects has not kept pace with increases in compensation of other workers in the construction industry as well as some of their professional brethren, including engineers, land surveyors, accountants and auditors.

For a variety of reasons, architects as a whole are unable to claim compensation appropriate to their role and commensurate with their responsibilities. The same points are always raised: so many years of education! demonstrable and unique expertise! a recognized, learned profession regulated by law! an activity entailing substantial legal and financial risks which in turn justify fair compensation and profits! Why then are so many architects apparently paid so poorly?

Supply and demand relationships are a major contributor to the problem, with too little work for too many architects. Architectural fees are frequently too low, or they go uncollected, flowing in unpredictable currents, just like projects. But why should fees be too low, given the architect's qualifications, risks, and efforts? The answer is competition. In the marketplace there is always pressure to quote fees that are at least comparable to the going rates, and

often to cut fees below the going rates, which then lowers the going rate another notch. Clients go shopping for architects and rarely hesitate to ask about cost of services. If a hungry architectural firm is anxious to secure a project commission, the temptation to propose a cut-rate fee can be overwhelming, even when it means cutting corners, compromising the quality of services, spending less time than needed, and paying slave wages to employees.

Many architectural practitioners feel trapped. On the one hand, as competent professionals they would like to invest all of the time and resources necessary to research thoroughly, discover, and describe the best possible design and to see that it is properly implemented. This implies that clients must share the architect's goals and visions and be willing to compensate them fully for the value of all required services. On the other hand, many architects' real-world experience teaches them that clients may view them as just another vendor among competing vendors, clients who believe architectural fees to be excessive yet want flawless, complete work at less than cost.

In the future it is unlikely that architects can expect to improve their earning power significantly without changing the supply-demand relationships and without insisting on full and adequate compensation, despite what the competition is doing. In a free market system the consumer of architectural services—and the architectural employer—will undoubtedly find sufficient numbers of warm bodies and firms eager and willing to work for the most minimal fee. No matter what price is proposed, there is always an architect somewhere who will do the work for less and promise as much or more.

To the established architect or firm, this situation is a mixed blessing. Although intense competition for projects makes it harder to survive, the ample supply of architects, both young and old, allows firms to keep their labor costs and fees as low as possible, since most architectural fee revenue is spent on staff salaries. In fact, the current economic structure of architectural practice depends on this exploitation of labor to provide services that are extremely labor intensive by their nature. A project can consume thousands of worker hours.

It is worth reminding ourselves, before concluding this discussion of compensation, that the points made are all relative. In other words, architects seem underpaid only when they are compared to certain others in our society. They can earn more than some people ever hope to earn and frequently earn more than teachers, scholars, musicians, actors, and artists doing work that may be equally creative and fulfilling. It is even possible to out-earn plumbers, truck drivers, attorneys, and doctors, if that is your goal as an architect—but it is not easy.

Ego Vulnerability: Getting Lost in the Crowd

The level of ego involvement in architecture is high, and this can lead to great frustration as well as provide the impetus for achieving. To most architects, succeeding means, among other things, gaining some measure of professional standing and reputation, if not fame. There is a natural craving for peer group recognition, even beyond one's clientele, for having done well, for being exceptional in some way.

Yet in actuality many architects feel, rightly or wrongly, that they have failed to gain the status or recognition they deserve. They toil away as employees, associates, or principals in firms, carrying on the demanding, day-to-day work of producing architecture, while a handful of their colleagues receive most of the attention and credit. Some perceive themselves as anonymous cogs in a giant system over which they have limited control. They feel unjustly treated and passed over.

Visit a large architectural office where there might be fifty or a hundred architects working. Many of them would characterize themselves as unfulfilled, underappreciated, underpaid, and overworked architects with lots of talent and little luck. Some feel exploited, chained to their workstations and jobs, unable to make that breakthrough to independence and even stardom. Most will have successfully completed professional educations, many will be licensed, and all will have differing but important forms of talent, indispensable to architectural practice. A few will feel cheated or deprived by external forces. Others will feel that they suffer from some combination of personal inadequacies that prevents them from doing or achieving more, resigning themselves to anonymity and content just to do their best. Still others will be dreaming and waiting for the right moment, the right opportunity, to emerge from the crowd.

The Risks of Envy

Why should architects feel or think this way? Why does this sound like a description of aspiring actors in New York or Hollywood rather than a group of highly trained, licensed professionals? Is this condition particularly acute in architecture? As the first chapter makes clear, fame and status, a kind of stardom or eminence, seem to be aspirations in architecture—and the lack thereof implies that one's work is incompetent, uninteresting, passé, or otherwise unworthy of notice. Hence there is an inescapable pressure on architects that motivates them but can also produce feelings of jealousy or envy. Professional jealousy can arise in all lines of work, but it may be more keenly felt in architecture. Given the competition and egos that prevail, it is easy to understand why architects fall victim to the sin of envy.

Envy and jealousy rarely surface in public. Instead, they are privately felt and coped with. They can appear whenever an architect observes some other architect winning while the observer is losing or is left out. They are beyond normal feelings of frustration or disappointment and can manifest themselves in a subtle but gnawing, slightly malicious way, sometimes accompanied by traces of ill will and resentment of the comparative success of others. Paradoxically, architects may have parallel feelings of respect and admiration for their envied competitors and peers. Professional jealousy is an unfortunate component of the architect's psyche, rarely acted on externally but capable of precipitating internal damage to the ego.

Anything can trigger such feelings, especially at moments of vulnerability: others busy when you are not; others winning awards or competitions when you are not; others being published or favorably reviewed when you are not; others being promoted when you are not; others making money when you are not. The negative stimuli can be unending. Losing a job or a commission you thought you should have gotten, or falling out of fashion as fashions change, can provoke and embitter. These sentiments are not restricted to young, immature, or unsuccessful architects. Every architect is susceptible, and, indeed, the higher one's aspirations, the higher the susceptibility.

Lack of Power and Influence

Some people seek more than professional and familial fulfillment in their careers and personal lives. They may aspire to gaining public recognition, prominence, power, and influence, wanting to be respected and admired by a constituency beyond their own professional colleagues and clients. They seek to be among the movers and shakers in their community, to be consulted on matters outside the realm of architecture. Perhaps invited to serve on important boards and commissions, they can help shape public policy.

If this is your inclination, then architecture might not be for you. Architects rarely achieve such status. Indeed, in American society, architects do enjoy some status as designers and technical specialists, but they seldom are among the prominent decision makers, typically politicians, attorneys, business owners, corporate and government executives, and people of great wealth. Regrettably, architects often are perceived as having narrow interests and expertise, limited primarily to matters of aesthetics and construction, even though many possess broad skills, knowledge, and wisdom. Architects themselves have reinforced this perception by frequently remaining aloof or uninvolved. Unfortunately, the relatively low public profile of architects, their minimal involvement in dealing with the larger society, is a persistent problem. Architecture is not a powerful profession.

Anxiety, Disappointment, and Depression

Professionally related depression is usually caused by failure or the prospect of failure. Lack or loss of work, financial setbacks, inadequate recognition, or adverse criticism can do the job. This suggests that to be a happy architect, you must be emotionally tough. Conversely, do not be an architect if you suffer from severe rejection anxiety or fear of failure, for periodic disappointments and failures are guaranteed in the profession of architecture.

Anxiety and depression over money matters are certainly not unique to architecture. But as professional designers, architects produce work that is continually scrutinized, tested, criticized, redone, and frequently rejected. Trite as it sounds, rejection comes with the territory. No one likes it, but architects must be especially able to accept and cope with it. This is not always easy.

Imagine the feelings that can well up when, after investing perhaps hundreds or thousands of hours in a design, you are told that your work is mediocre, unacceptable, or, worse, terrible. Rejection, disappointment, and failure are bitter medicines to swallow, but every architect has tasted them, no matter how unjustifiably.

Rejection does not mean necessarily that extraordinary talent and effort have not been applied in creating an architectural design. Brilliant labors of love are rejected all the time, along with mediocre ones. However, judgment of architecture can be highly subjective, based on the values and taste of those who are judging. Judgments are made for political, social, and economic reasons totally beyond the architect's powers of anticipation and control, so the architect has little choice but to endure these recurring circumstances, always exerting his or her best, or to drop out.

Dropping out may appear to be the best alternative for avoiding depression if compensating successes prove unattainable.

Personal Encumbrances

Architecture demands taking risks. It demands great investment of time, effort, and emotional and physical energy to achieve anything worthwhile. To be able to seize opportunities when they arise or pursue unconventional goals requires both personal resources and a certain freedom from personal encumbrances.

In particular, establishing an architectural firm is often a great risk, especially financially. Yet it is the objective of most architects starting out in practice after school, an objective only some will reach. If an architect is supporting a family through his or her job, with no other substantial sources of income or assets, then giving up a regular and reliable salary to venture forth as an independent practitioner can be a bit daunting.

Traveling and additional graduate study are other pursuits that can be extremely beneficial to an architect. They too are difficult to accomplish if one is overly encumbered with dependents, debts, or doubts. Obviously those who begin with a financial support system or are personally unencumbered have a distinct advantage. Inheriting money or being married to a working, supportive spouse helps. And teaching architecture can provide both time and income for young, aspiring architects to begin practices while teaching.

An architect for whom I once worked gave me some memorable advice as I was departing my summer job to return to architectural school. After calling me into his office to say farewell, he pointed his finger toward the drafting room, then occupied by about a dozen architects bent over their drawing boards, and proposed that I should keep one thing in mind if I did not want to end up like them: don't marry or have kids too soon! He was really saying that if I wanted to travel or start a practice someday too many premature commitments could stand in the way. Financial and personal obstacles can keep architects laboring away in drafting rooms.

Lack of Talent

Some people fail because they lack talent. Or they do not meet all of their goals because they do not have the essential resources needed to do so. Aspiring architects should consider this possibility. If some of the key intellectual, emotional, and personal attributes noted in the preceding chapter are missing, architecture can be an uphill endeavor, even for very intelligent people. Every year teachers of architecture see bright students who nevertheless seem to be pursuing the wrong career because their aptitudes clearly lie elsewhere. Some are uncomfortable or awkward with drawing and graphics. Others lack analytic and technical ability. Still others show little creativity, imagination, or visual sensitivity. These can be serious impediments for those who desire to be an architect.

Being intelligent is no guarantee of aptitude for architecture. A large dose of native talent must lie in the genes; talents can be brought forth and nurtured but not taught. Like certain personal qualities, such talent may be developed in spite of, not because of, formal education. Intuition, instinct, and inventiveness are indispensable to architectural design; erudition and intelligence are necessary but not sufficient.

Lack of Passion and Dedication

Also indispensable to achieving success in architecture are frequently extraordinary levels of passion, dedication, and effort. Without them, the prospective or practicing architect surely faces rejection and failure. Since architecture is so demanding of time and energy, unwillingness to work hard, and to accept often minimal rewards, is a sound reason not to be an architect.

Students first discover this truism in architectural school. Being very labor intensive, requiring countless hours of mental and manual effort making drawings and crafting physical and computer-based models, architectural study prepares one for what is to come: lots more hard work and always the potential for rejection.

Those fully committed to their work and impassioned about their professional mission benefit from a sort of religious sense of purpose that inspires them and helps them weather the rougher moments. Virtually all accomplished architects throughout history have been motivated above all by love of design.

Legal and Financial Risks

Architects who own firms and whose designs get built are exposed to substantial legal and financial risks. The major legal risk, professional negligence, can cause clients or others to suffer monetary damages. Architects are sued regularly by plaintiffs who believe the architect committed an error leading to injury or financial loss to the plaintiff. When such claims are made against an architect, whether groundless or not, the architect may be forced to compensate the plaintiff for some portion of the alleged damages following negotiations, arbitration, or litigation. And no matter what the outcome, substantial legal fees usually have to be paid.

Like others in our society who perform so-called personal services (physicians, attorneys, dentists, engineers), architects assume professional negligence liability personally, as individuals. They cannot protect their assets by incorporating. They can purchase insurance that will cover most of the costs of defending and settling negligence claims, but the insurance is costly.

Even with insurance, negotiating, litigating, and settling claims is intrusive, time-consuming, and stressful. Claims and litigation have increased because of rising, often unrealistic expectations held by clients and consumers, leading them to sue architects even when there is little or no evidence of architectural wrongdoing. Thus, an architect may be slapped with a lawsuit despite his or her innocence. Furthermore the very existence of insurance invites lawsuits. If architects were both impoverished and uninsured, they would rarely be sued.

Another unfortunate consequence of the rising tide of litigation is the increased practice of defensive design and excessive documentation—the creation of a paper trail—that presumably protects the architect against the ever-present threat of lawsuits. But this induces architects to be less innovative, to stick to the tried and true, and to devote more time to being pseudolawyers instead of designers. If you want to avoid the minefield of liability and litigation, then architectural practice is unsafe ground unless you remain forever an employee.

Financially, there is an even greater risk than being sued for professional negligence: the risk of not being paid for services rendered and having to take legal action to collect fees. Potentially the architect can suffer loss of income as well as time, to which may be added the stress of proving the case since, as plaintiff, the architect must assume the burden of proof. Here the real victors are the lawyers.

Disillusionment

The roadblocks, risks, and uncertainties already identified produce frustration and disillusionment—perhaps the greatest overall risk in becoming an architect. When architects have met the demands of professional preparation, paid their proverbial dues, mustered their talents, and then found their aspirations and ideals compromised or their ideas rejected, disillusionment may set in. Usually there is not even the offsetting consolation of having made a lot of money. In fact architects say that they sometimes feel like whores, working in a profession where prostituting one's goals and standards is commonplace. A dim view indeed.

Architects periodically feel exploited or used. They sometimes provide services for little or no pay, hoping for something in the future but ending up with nothing. Many see their career as a giant compromise, having given more than they got and accepted less than they deserved. How different, they say to themselves in retrospect, than what they imagined when they first put pencil to paper in a design studio. Some accept this condition as part of the business of architecture. They find sufficient rewards to offset the disappointments, or they may even be able to disregard the problems altogether. A few abandon the profession, seeking firmer ground.

One thing is certain: for anyone contemplating or just starting a career in architecture, there is no way to predict where the choice will lead. Undoubtedly there will be both rewards and frustrations, moments of delight and depression. The prospective architect can only hope that the sum of the assets will exceed the sum of the liabilities, yielding a positive net worth.

II

Becoming an Architect

3

The Structure of Architectural Education

Architectural education, for many architects, is among the most stimulating, challenging, and formative periods of their entire careers. It also can be among the most frustrating, a period of trial and error, of discovery and questioning. To understand what becoming an architect entails, let us first explore the organization and structure of architectural education in the United States.

There are over one hundred architectural schools (see the list in the appendix) in North America, most of which are members of the Association of Collegiate Schools of Architecture (ACSA). In the United States, their professional degree programs, whether undergraduate or graduate, are accredited by the National Architectural Accrediting Board (NAAB), which periodically visits all such schools to ensure that they are meeting stipulated criteria for conducting programs in architecture. Criteria address such issues as faculty qualifications, physical facilities, budget, curricula and course content, and overall program goals. These same criteria are of great interest to prospective students of architecture.

Almost all architectural programs are constituent parts of universities, existing either as departments or schools within university divisions or colleges. This linkage is appropriate because the discipline of architecture is close to many other university-based disciplines—art, engineering, physics and mathematics, computer science, history, horticulture, geography, sociology—and would suffer measurably if isolated from the diverse academic components of a university. Further, courses in architecture are themselves of interest to students and faculty in other departments on university campuses.

Most states have public universities offering programs and degrees in architecture, and many private universities have architectural schools. Two-year community colleges have begun teaching prearchitecture courses for students planning to enroll eventually in accredited, university degree programs. There are very few wholly independent schools of architecture unaffiliated with major universities. (One of the most successful of these is the Boston Architectural Center, known as the BAC, which offers a unique, accredited, cooperative program.)

American architectural schools offer several different types of degree programs, the source of considerable confusion for prospective architectural students.

Program Types

Type 1 is an undergraduate, four-year program leading to a B.S. or B.A. degree that is *not* an accredited professional degree. Many schools offer this program. After earning these degrees, students must usually spend at least two more years in a graduate program to earn an accredited, professional degree, in most cases a master of architecture (M.Arch.). Also, prior to entering architecture graduate school, many students take off a year or two to work. This type of program allows students to test the waters of architecture without an excessive investment of time, in the event that they change their minds. Such preprofessional programs may provide up to half of a complete architectural curriculum.

Type 2—an undergraduate, five-year program leading to the B.Arch. degree—is an accredited professional degree. This was once the norm for architectural education in the United States, and many schools have retained this program despite the shift to graduate architectural education since the 1960s. Its advantages are less cost—five years of college versus six or seven, undergraduate tuition fees versus graduate tuition fees (almost always higher)—

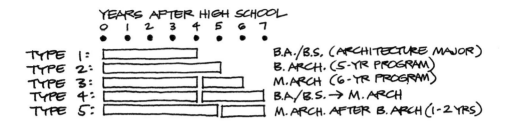

YEARS AFTER HIGH SCHOOL
0 1 2 3 4 5 6 7

TYPE 1: — B.A./B.S. (ARCHITECTURE MAJOR)
TYPE 2: — B. ARCH. (5-YR PROGRAM)
TYPE 3: — M. ARCH (6-YR PROGRAM)
TYPE 4: — B.A./B.S. → M. ARCH
TYPE 5: — M. ARCH. AFTER B. ARCH (1-2 YRS)

and academic continuity from freshman to fifth year. It immerses students in architecture when they are very young and therefore most receptive to new ideas and experimentation. Its disadvantages are that it compresses both professional and general education together into an intense five-year period, often precluding exploration through elective studies in other fields; it forces an early career choice, normally at the freshman or sophomore year levels when many eighteen- or nineteen-year-old students are still maturing and questing; and once begun, it is usually an all-or-nothing program, since the B.Arch. can be earned only upon the completion of all five years of study.

Type 3—a graduate, professional degree program leading to the M.Arch—is for students who have already earned an undergraduate, nonprofessional B.A. or B.S. degree (type 1) with a major in architecture. These are two- to three-year programs for those without an accredited professional degree (a B.Arch. or M.Arch.). Students in these programs enroll as graduate students, and they may hold undergraduate degrees from the same university in which they are enrolling as graduate students.

Type 4—a graduate program leading to the first, accredited degree in architecture, usually the M.Arch. degree—is for students holding undergraduate degrees in majors other than architecture. Such programs enroll students only as graduate students and normally require three to four years of intensive, graduate-level studies in architecture. Students in these programs are generally assumed to have had little architectural preparation prior to entering the program. Typically these programs are populated by older students—some returning to school after working or establishing families—with degrees in the arts and humanities, engineering, science, business, or social sciences.

Type 5 encompasses graduate programs leading to second, post-professional degrees in architecture for students already holding a B.Arch. or M.Arch. degree. Although a few Ph.D. degree programs exist, almost all postprofessional degree programs are at the master's level, with a specific topic or area of study specified. Advanced master's degree programs in architecture may vary from one to two years in duration, depending on the school and area of study.

The lack of national consistency in programs and names of degrees reflects the independent nature of individual architectural schools, coupled with the reluctance of the architectural establishment—those in practice and in education—to standardize architectural programs. The NAAB, which certifies architectural school programs, has established program evaluation criteria, but these pertain primarily to the subject matter it expects all programs to cover. It does not prescribe curricula, courses, or teaching approaches. Rather, it asks each school to define its own specific goals, standards, and methods and then evaluates its success in meeting its own objectives, along with verifying that key subjects are addressed and resources are adequate. Although there are some generally accepted notions of what constitutes a legitimate architectural program, schools nevertheless enjoy wide latitude in designing courses and curricula. Consequently, reading names of degrees and courses in catalogs reveals little of the quality and specifics of a school's program.

Curricular Content

Despite nominal variations in packaging of courses and curricula from one architectural school to another, there is nevertheless substantial commonality in content. Therefore what follows is not a description of the specific form of architectural school curricula but is rather a summary of their basic content. A course may have dozens of different names from one school to another, so it is imperative to focus on subject matter instead of labeling. Further the exact chronology of subjects offered in schools varies slightly, but again these variations are less significant than the overall sequence, which is fairly uniform.

Most school curricula require the cumulative equivalent of eight fifteen-week semesters of architectural studies, which can be a mix of undergraduate and graduate work, for successful completion of a professional degree program. A few graduate schools do it in six semesters (program type 4). With no previous background in architecture, you should assume that completing your first professional degree program takes approximately five to eight calendar years after high school, depending on when you enter architectural school.

The structure and content of architectural programs are divided generally into three broad areas: design, history and theory, and technology. The majority of courses in any architectural school catalog deal explicitly with subject matter and exercises in one of these three areas, although there can be overlaps. Design necessarily considers history and technology. History of architecture is the study of the history of building and city design related to cultural, political, social, and technological history. Technology courses teach students theories and methods for carrying out architectural design concepts. This interrelation of areas of specialty is the keystone of the discipline of architecture, itself an amalgamation of disciplines.

Design

Courses in design must usually be taken in every semester of any architectural program. They are the unifying element, the primary pedagogical activity that brings together all the diverse contributing disciplines and concerns in architecture. Design studio courses typically account for 35 to 40 percent of the total credit hours needed in architecture, and they may actually consume a disproportionately higher percentage of students' time—perhaps from 50 to 60 percent.

Integral to the study of design is the study of fundamental principles and techniques of architectural representation and composition. These include the following:

Freehand drawing Sketching of forms, real or imagined, in two or three dimensions to develop eye-hand facility using different media (pencil and ink primarily but also charcoal, pastels, watercolor, or other paint) and techniques for making lines, tones, textures, and shading; and to learn to produce sketches rapidly, comfortably, and with some accuracy—one of the architect's most invaluable skills.

Constructed drawing Representing form through the construction of drawings using drafting tools: orthogonal projections (plan, elevation, section), paraline or axonometric drawing, perspective drawing (one-, two-, and three-point perspectives), and shadow projection. The essential tools are the scale (for measuring to translate real, full-scale dimensions into proportional, scaled-down dimensions in drawings), the straightedge (a T-square or parallel bar), triangles, compass and divider, curves, erasing shield, and last, but not least, erasers. Along with mastering manual drafting techniques, students also learn how to create constructed drawings using computers.

Presentation graphics Manual and computer-based methods of rendering drawings and preparing presentations; composing drawing formats and titles; selecting media and paper or board; creating washes, tones, textures, shading, and shadowing; collage; representing structures, furniture, vegetation, people, and vehicles; the selection and control of line weights; and the building of models.

Visual composition and analysis Using graphic techniques and a variety of media to invent or manipulate forms in two or three dimensions or to analyze existing forms. The objects of study can be abstract or real for purposes of inventing form, and the forms analyzed can be buildings, cities, manufactured artifacts, vegetation, painting, or sculpture. The goal is to discover patterns and principles of composition.

The major component of the design menu is the architectural *design studio*, where students carry out research and design for specific projects. In the first year of design, projects are usually abstract and conceptual. In subsequent years, projects are often analogous to what architects do in practice: designing buildings in

landscapes or cities, complexes of buildings, parts of cities or suburbs, and even entire settlements or towns.

The architectural design studio operates fairly consistently
throughout the United States. Typically, there are from twelve to
eighteen students for each design studio instructor, the studio critic, and each critic's section may be one of several at a given level
within the curriculum. The studio critic may operate independently, doing his or her own projects and following his or her own
schedule. Or the studio may be part of a coordinated effort involving several sections, an entire level, or even the entire school. This
too can change from semester to semester within a school.

Design studio teachers normally plan the studio course, select projects, schedule work, and evaluate their students' progress. Studio
courses have the greatest amount of student-teacher contact in the
curriculum, and more than most other courses in any university.
They are ordinarily six- to nine-credit courses (typical lecture or
seminar courses are three credits) and meet three or four days each
week for three to four hours per day. This means twelve to sixteen
hours of in-class work and interaction weekly. Part of this time is
spent working independently, part getting critiques of your work
at your desk ("desk crits"), and part evaluating work in group
reviews or pinups.

Generally studio design projects increase in complexity as the student progresses through the program. Complexity depends on the
number and difficulty of design issues addressed in a given
project, not necessarily on a project's size or cost. A house could be
a more complex project than an office building or industrial plant,
depending on site conditions and design requirements, and uncon-
strained design problems can be more challenging than highly
constrained ones.

In most programs, beginning-year studio projects tend to be basic
and focused, concentrating on design fundamentals. Students are
introduced to visual composition in two and three dimensions,
concepts of spatial and functional organization, circulation, and
structural behavior. Projects may be theoretical rather than practical

A student presenting a studio design project
for review by a jury.

in nature, independent of building design, to encourage abstract, creative thinking and to reinforce graphic and representational skills.

Projects in the following semesters become more and more like architecture, although specific requirements and conditions may still be idealized and unrealistic. Projects that illustrate this approach include small pavilions or kiosks, vacation homes or retreats (usually in the mountains or the woods, if not on the beach), churches, and modest civic buildings such as a branch library or movie theater. Each project may be presented by the critic to introduce the student to new design issues while reinforcing principles already learned. One project might emphasize site planning and building massing (shaping a building's overall volume on a site), another might deal with structure, materials, and climate, and still another might focus on facade composition. In all projects, the student must be concerned with the creation and manipulation of spaces, volumes, surfaces, and structures on a chosen site in response to a stipulated set of design requirements, called the project program.

As students' competency increases, they advance into higher-level design studios, where they explore design projects with more complicated site and program requirements and opportunities for more sophisticated investigation of theoretical questions and architectural technology. Programmatically, such projects can include housing, health facilities, complex public or administrative buildings, schools or religious centers, theaters, commercial facilities, libraries, museums, or transportation terminals. More rigorous site planning occurs, with some projects entailing the design of neighborhoods, city blocks, streetscapes, town or city centers, transportation corridors, public parks, and even residential subdivisions.

The last semester of design frequently involves a thesis. This may require research and preparation in the preceding semester, during which the student selects a topic or project and gathers the data needed to undertake the design. Most thesis work is done independently, unlike the preceding design studios in which students work together and see their instructors two or three times per week. Thesis students normally have an adviser or advisory committee of faculty who may review the student's progress only four or five times before the final presentation. Some schools require submission of a written thesis document, especially at the master's level, which must include photoreductions of final drawings and models.

Almost all architectural schools have adopted minimum standards of competency and performance that students must meet before advancing to the next level of design studio or before graduation. Since the design studio sequence is continuous throughout most programs, it is not unusual to find studio sections with students who did not all begin architectural school at the same time. Many take extra time to complete architectural school for academic and personal reasons (such as finances).

History and Theory

History and theory, the second broad area of study within any architectural program, is concerned with the past but also impinges vitally on the present and future. By studying history, the prospective architect learns the who, what, when, where, how, and why of what has gone before. Looking at architectural precedents, coupled with reading the many texts on architecture theory written by historians and architects, discloses ideas, beliefs, and principles relevant to what architects do today and will do tomorrow. The study of history and theory introduces the architect to his or her legacy and suggests how that legacy might be applicable to the present and future.

The historical evolution of architecture and architectural theory may be approached chronologically, geographically, and thematically. In other words, the historian may consider the development of architecture by time periods (decades, centuries, or eras), by location (cities, regions, cultures, countries, or continents), or by specific topics of interest (focusing on styles, architects, technology, symbology, philosophy, or building types, for example). Each historian in each school has a special way of thinking about and presenting architectural history and theory, but again there is substantial commonality in content. Following is a representative, though inevitably incomplete, list of course content in architectural history and theory:

• Surveys of Western architectural history and literature from ancient to modern (usually fast, focusing on major historical periods and illustrated with countless numbers of slides)

• Surveys of non-Western architecture, primarily Islamic and Far Eastern cultures (These surveys are much rarer than those covering Western history.)

• Ancient Western architectural history, concentrating on Egypt, the Near East, Greece, and Rome

• Early Christian and Byzantine architecture

- Architecture of the Middle Ages, primarily the Gothic in France, Italy, and England
- The Renaissance, primarily in Italy
- Architectural history and theory between the Renaissance and the industrial revolution—the baroque and rococo periods in Europe, and neoclassicism in France and England
- The French beaux arts influence from the eighteenth to the twentieth century
- American architecture in the nineteenth and twentieth centuries
- Modern and postmodern American architecture
- Modern European architecture, usually divided into pre–World War I, between the wars, and post–World War II periods
- Russian architecture
- Japanese architecture
- History of indigenous architectures (usually across diverse regional, cultural, temporal, and technological lines)
- History of architectural theory
- History of building technology
- History of landscape architecture
- History and theory of urban design, exploring the origins, form, and planning principles related to towns, cities, and urban spaces

No one school covers all of these subjects in its collection of history courses, and no student can begin to study but a fraction of the topics on this list. Survey courses, lasting one or two semesters, skim the surface of the past, whereas smaller lecture or seminar courses provide the opportunity to concentrate on the subsequently listed topics. Once in school, you will quickly uncover your interests and learn which teachers and courses appeal to you.

Like related courses in the humanities, history and theory courses in architectural school consist of assigned and recommended reading, coupled with extensive viewing of slides selected and projected by the lecturer or seminar leader (who may sometimes be a student in the class). Essays, term papers, and small projects are usually assigned. Depending on the school's location and resources, teachers may lead students on field trips. Indeed, field trips are popular in studio and technology courses as well.

Technology

Technology categorizes the third type of architectural course work found in all professional school curricula. It encompasses subjects dealing with how designs are implemented, with principles and methods of construction and environmental control. Ideally technology should not be thought of as separate and different from design. Instead, it is a label for courses that are more closely associated with science, engineering, and management, as to both content and method.

Within the sphere of architectural technology there are five sub-technologies: structural technology, construction materials and methods, environmental control technology, computer-aided design (CAD) technology, and management or business technology. Some of each is required in all architectural schools, although in differing doses and with widely ranging levels of rigor. Further, like design and history, some architectural technology subjects are covered by examinations given by states for the licensing of architects. And the essential subject matter in architectural technology is more easily understood by aspiring architects who have some knowledge of mathematics and physics, a reason many schools require beginning students to take introductory calculus and physics.

Structures

The study of structural concepts is indispensable for anyone who hopes to design and build buildings. Structure is that part of a building, or any other constructed form, that provides support. The structure resists the loads of gravity (weight), wind, earth movement, and other forces that may be applied to the structure at any time. Some of these loads act vertically, such as gravity, and some horizontally or laterally, such as wind or earthquake forces. Architects also refer to the structure of a building as the building skeleton or frame, and in certain structures, walls, floors, and roofs constitute integral elements of the framing system. Any element that contributes to the stability of a structure under conditions of loading becomes a member of the structural frame or system.

Obviously many components of a building are not part of the building's structural system—its plumbing and its windows, for example. Not so obvious, however, is the role that the structural system plays in affecting, or being affected by, the overall spatial and volumetric form of a building. First, the structure must be designed to work safely and efficiently in supporting and stabilizing the building. Second, the architect must orchestrate both the patterns of framing and the patterns of architectural form (volume, space, surface) to create visual and constructional relationships.

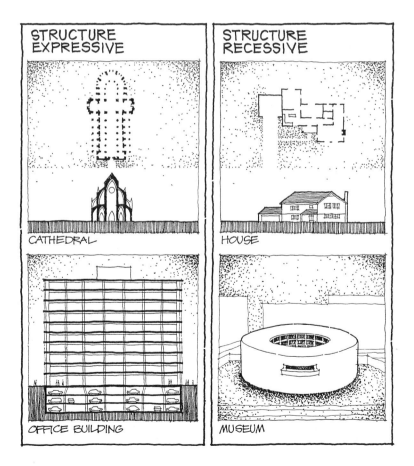

Here is clearly the interface between the technology of structure and the art of design. Indeed, the architect can use the structural system expressionistically, creating a visual language of exposed structural elements and details. Or the architect can make the structural system recessive, concealing it from direct view.

To master this, students in architectural school study statics (forces on bodies in equilibrium), strengths of materials (how specific materials behave under stress), and the behavior of fundamental structural components—beams, columns, cables, rods, footings and foundations, bearing walls, and slabs or decks—when forces are applied to them. They learn about stresses and strains, deflection, bending, buckling, tension and compression, all of which occur when elements of a structure are loaded. They also learn about connections and joints between members, about temperature-dependent expansion and contraction, and about entire structural systems (for example, how entire building frames behave when loaded). Such systems include the familiar balloon frame of a house, post-and-beam framing typical of office buildings, bearing wall construction, membrane or tensile structures (such as tents or bridges), thin shell structures (plates, vaults, domes), trusses, space frames, and others.

I do not mean to suggest that architects are expected to engineer in detail the structural frame of buildings they design. Rather, architects in practice rely on structural engineers for the specific design of all load-bearing components of buildings. Nevertheless, architects must know the fundamentals so they can guide and understand the engineer's work, and contribute directly to critical decision making regarding the look, quality, and cost of a structural system.

Materials and Methods of Construction

Beyond structural systems architects must know the implications of using the primary structural materials: wood, steel, and concrete. Each material has unique characteristics, both structurally and aesthetically, and the architect must choose materials and systems thoughtfully and knowledgeably. Strength, durability, workability, weight, resistance to heat and weather, and cost are among the

properties considered. In school, students also may be introduced to other materials as well—glass, metals other than steel, plastics, fibers, and composites.

Although it is common practice to rely on structural engineers for the final design of structural systems, the architect retains primary responsibility for determining and designing the details of assembly for nonstructural building components. Some schools teach theory and practice of detailed design (detailing) in specialized courses that develop knowledge about the performance of materials and manufactured components. Here the designer is concerned with the control of moisture, heat loss and gain, dimensional stability, durability, availability and cost of labor and materials, sustainability (related to energy and natural resource conservation), and appearance. The architect must show in design drawings how pieces fit together, how joints and connections are made, and what the dimensions of all assembled components will be. Typical details depict roof, wall, and floor assemblies, window and door assemblies, railings, stairs, cabinetry, and decorative finishing elements.

Environmental Controls

Studies in environmental control technology are concerned with making the built environment comfortable and usable for human occupancy. They are also concerned with the use and conservation of energy within buildings. With the help of engineering specialists, architects must fashion ambient environments that are safe from fire, offer thermal comfort (neither too cold or too hot), are properly lighted, provide fresh, unpolluted air to breathe, and have appropriate acoustic characteristics. In an era of expensive energy, buildings must be well insulated, retaining and reusing heat while capturing the sun's energy in winter.

In addition to tempering the environment and satisfying the senses, architects and their consultants must design systems for distributing energy, fluids, gases, goods, and people within buildings. These systems are like metabolic networks woven into the rigid, supporting skeleton of a building's body. Students of architecture study the basics of electrical systems, plumbing systems, heating and cooling systems, ventilating systems, and conveying systems (elevators and escalators). They learn both engineering principles and specific applications, understanding how such systems influence overall building design. As with structural systems, architectural designers generally do not undertake the detailed, quantitative design of environmental control systems but rather collaborate with engineering experts in system selection and design coordination.

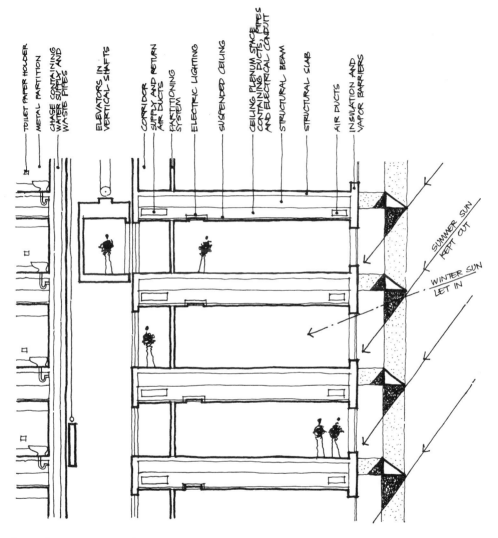

Some of the systems and elements that shape, serve and control buildings and the spaces within.

Many schools offer courses that cover lighting, both natural and electrical, and acoustics. Students may study room acoustics, the behavior and perception of sound within spaces, and sound transmission (the passage of sound between spaces or through structures). Anyone who has functioning eyes and ears knows that the world is full of architecture where sight and sound are difficult, if not impossible.

Computer-Aided Design

Virtually every architecture school in North America has a computer lab for students, and a few even have computer terminals in or near design studio spaces. Some schools require every student to have a personal computer capable of connecting to a local area network, either within the school or campus-wide. Computer technology has become a powerful tool not only for practicing architects, but also for architecture students and faculty. Accordingly, most schools offer computer-aided design (CAD) courses as electives, and because architecture firms prefer hiring CAD-literate graduates, increasing numbers of schools require some level of CAD mastery.

Today many students entering architecture school already have acquired basic computer skills. Therefore, CAD courses in architecture concentrate primarily on teaching students how to use specialized software programs to build and test three-dimensional, computer-based models of their design concepts, along with plotting conventional architectural drawings. Employing state-of-the-art programs, students can generate complex perspectives and axonometrics from many viewpoints. They also can study structural behavior, lighting design, colors, materials, surface textures, and even acoustic characteristics of a proposed building or space. And students with access to very high-speed, large-memory computers can produce animated videos simulating walk-throughs or fly-bys in real time.

As powerful and useful as computers have become, they remain just a tool to aid design. Designers still must make all the judgments necessary to create, develop, and communicate design ideas. Consequently, most schools insist that despite available and ever-changing computer technology, students must continue to learn basic manual design skills, including drawing.

Management

Management, the fifth subtopic under technology, is somewhat of a catchall. It embraces those topics and courses that prepare students to conduct the business affairs and operational tasks of architecture. Included are courses that address business administration, methods of practice, finance and economics, legal concerns, and construction management. Schools vary greatly in the number and variety of such courses taught, with some offering very few. They may rely on courses given in other departments (business administration, economics, computer science, or civil engineering) to satisfy students' needs and interests.

Almost all architectural schools teach at least one course about professional architectural practice. These courses explain how firms are organized and managed. They delve into marketing of services, fees and compensation, project management and documentation, contracts, legal and ethical concerns, and construction administration. More advanced courses focused on the management of construction projects are offered in a few architectural schools. These deal with planning and scheduling of construction tasks, coordination of building trades and subcontractors, estimating and bidding, materials purchasing, contract negotiating, and cost accounting. However, many schools of architecture have resisted introducing this subject matter which, to some, appears to be invading the territory of the general contractor. They would argue that construction management belongs more appropriately in schools of management or engineering.

Several schools teach real estate economics. Such courses examine the sources of capital for building, the development process through which buildings are created, the economic characteristics of projects built in both the private and public sectors, and the role of government in architecture—its regulations, zoning and building codes, tax and investment laws, planning policy, and construction programs.

Electives

Courses in design, history, and technology are the core of an architectural curriculum, but that core should be complemented by electives in other areas of study. Indeed, electives may be required. They broaden professional education and may furnish credit hours needed for graduation. Some architectural courses, particularly in history or technology, can be taken as electives when they are not part of the core requirements. Electives outside architecture may offer the largest and most fertile selection, however, reinforcing the liberal-professional duality of architectural education.

Following are courses or topics most relevant to the study and practice of architecture. Again, the list is inevitably incomplete.

Urban planning

Geography

Horticulture and landscape architecture

Anthropology and archaeology

Art

Sociology

Psychology

Economics

Business administration and management science

Civil engineering

History

Government and politics

The discussion of curricular content should make clear why schools of architecture are integral constituents of universities, in contrast to law or medical schools. The latter, though attached to universities, tend to operate independently, with little academic interaction between the professional school and the rest of the university community. Nevertheless, architectural schools do develop their own conspicuous, iconoclastic identities within the university setting. And, architectural school applicants and students must create their own identities.

4

Experiencing Architectural School

No outline of the structure of architectural education in the United States can ever reveal what it is really like to be an architectural student. This chapter offers an account of the educational journey, I hope the next best thing to being there.

The First Year and Work Load Shock

The first year of immersion in architectural school is an encounter, a mystery and a surprise, a period marked by extraordinary rates of learning coupled with extraordinary fatigue. No matter how well prepared you are or what you have been told, it will be different from what you expected. The real first year is that year when you are enrolled in the beginning studio design courses while taking other architectural courses as well. You will be very, very busy.

In fact, one of the first shocks is how busy you will be—the work load shock. Few students, whether from high school or college, anticipate the amount of work piled on in architectural school, especially in first year. It seems to be a tradition, one of many, for the first-year introductory design studio to set the initial pace. That pace is incredibly hectic and intense, with steady, unending assignments of variable duration. Some require hours, some days, others weeks (often broken down into shorter subassignments). The staccato rhythm of basic design projects demands constant effort, day and night at times, far beyond the credit hour allotment that catalogs cite.

The work load shock, like any other assault on the mind and body, produces both positive and negative responses. Negatively, it is tiring, enervating, and numbing. Much of the studio work is labor intensive rather than intellect intensive. Hours are spent drawing or crafting. Some of these hours will seem tedious and others exhilarating. Up moments are later wiped out by down moments as the struggle to keep going and keep abreast, let alone ahead, goes on. Second winds, fueled by bursts of adrenaline and surges of renewed strength and energy, recur with reasonable frequency. If you can tolerate it all, it will toughen you.

Part of coping with work load shock is time management. With the design studio demanding so much time and energy, how does anyone meet other obligations? There seems to be a deadline every other day and some days two or three. Lulls are few and far between. The faculty will usually tell you that you should simply try to work steadily and regularly in each subject, allocating your time to each course continuously throughout the semester. Easier said than done.

Much of the work is produced in intense spurts, usually just before deadlines. The creative process defies attempts at smoothness, continuity, and regularity. Architects refer to such spurts as *charrettes*. The charrette, a French word meaning "little cart," applies to any intense, uninterrupted period of work prior to a deadline, almost always including at least one all-night stand. (Many years ago, at the Ecole des Beaux Arts in Paris, a charrette would arrive to collect project drawings just prior to the final deadline, and students, desperate to finish, would climb aboard the moving cart still adding last-minute touches to their drawings—hence the term *en charrette*.) If you visit an architectural school studio, especially near the end of a semester, you will see students on charrette day and night. Many never go home. Some practically live in the studio in what can best be described as camping-out conditions.

The most sensible attitude for handling first-year work loads is a positive, have fun, on-to-victory one. *Illegitimus non carborundum,* interpreted liberally to mean "Don't let the bastards grind you down!" Hang in, be tough, enjoy the occasional psychic pain and degradation as well as the periodic successes and endless enlightenment. Amaze your friends and family with your dedication and ability to overcome. Other students in the university will be awed by your commitment and endurance. Rare is the campus where architecture students are not considered the most hardworking, grind-it-out students or where architecture is not considered one of the hardest majors.

You will find little sympathy among most faculty when you air complaints about the amount of work you have to do, the overlapping deadlines and exams, the pressures, and the state of your mental and physical health. Their lack of sympathy does not mean that they do not understand or appreciate what you are experiencing. They have been through it too. They know that you are behind in sleep, neglecting your friends or family, in desperate need of a bath, and probably going broke while trying to pay your way through school. They know that your love life is suffering or interfering with your work. But they will tell you it is inevitable, a taste of and preparation for future reality. It is a rite of passage, a deposit on account for the dues anyone must pay to become an architect. The work load and its pressures are a positive stimulus as well as an ordeal.

New Values, New Language

The work load shock is accompanied by the value and language shocks. The latter results from being suddenly deluged by a new vocabulary. It is also an imprecise vocabulary. Only architects and a few architectural groupies really know the lingo. Indeed, there are sublingos that are accessible only to a minority of architects. You will first hear the language from your teachers, then from upper-level students and others who read the architectural media and architectural books.

Value shock is related to language shock because values are professed and examined through language. To appreciate value shock, you must accept the notion, a priori, that all academic or professional fields have elaborately developed, internal value systems: a set of commonly understood criteria or standards by which people and their work are measured within the field. This set of values and criteria, like its concomitant vocabulary, is not clearly written down anywhere. You cannot go out and buy a book titled *Architecture's Value System: How to Judge Everything You See or Hear* or *Words Architects Use and What They Mean.*

The values and vocabulary of architecture in school come as a shock because, first, they are unfamiliar; second, they are unclear and ambiguous; and third, their application and meaning is context dependent, changing from person to person or week to week. Just when you thought you had begun to figure out what your teacher was talking about, new metaphors and references renew your confusion.

Architecture is at once an art and a science. It demands logic, method, rational analysis, and measurable quantification, on the one hand, and intuition, emotion, sentiment, willfulness, and subjective judgment on the other. Thus the beginning student faces continual conflict, uncertainty, and confusion, especially in the design studio where values and judgments that cannot be justified scientifically are routinely presented, debated, and defended. Students discover that design thinking occurs on both sides of the brain. Accordingly, design teachers expect work that simultaneously exhibits sound reasoning and aesthetic invention.

Since most architecture students share traditional secondary and college academic experiences, they also share similar expectations when they embark on a new subject in a new course: the teacher presents specific material and asks specific questions, and the student periodically regurgitates, often with minimum digestion, what has been presented. Emphasis was always on finding answers, on deriving solutions. The student longs to know what the teacher "wants." "Tell us!" say the students, "and we'll give it to you."

Yet the values espoused by design studio critics may seem vague, the pedagogical expectations ill defined. One day the critic says

that it is important to think about efficient and legible circulation, and the next day the critic protests that the design is too much like a circulation diagram: too little color one day, too much the next. Nice proportions, proclaims the critic, but it doesn't work; or it works, but the proportions are bad. Be simple, they say, too simple-minded, they say. It has wonderful complexity . . . it's too complex . . . it lacks complexity. Less is more. You can't read the structure. Why express the structure? Too much variety! Too little variety!

Perhaps the intertwining of values and vocabulary is becoming apparent. What about these words we teachers utter so often, so confidently, so critically? What do we mean, and what do we really want? How do teachers, much less beginning students, know when a proportion is bad, or which colors to use, or when there is just the right amount of complexity? Obviously, claim the students, the critics know something—some set of understood but not explicitly communicated values—that allows them to make judgments and to know the truth. Why not share it?

Words expressing values pour forth. Buildings are described as "constructs," "habitable artifacts," "environments," "built form," "structures," or "edifices." They can be "object" (free-standing), "background," or "in-fill" buildings." The word "space" can refer to a room, a corridor or hallway, a street, a plaza, an attic, an interval, or any void. Space can "flow," "penetrate," "articulate," "modulate," "expand," or "contract." It can be amorphous and open,

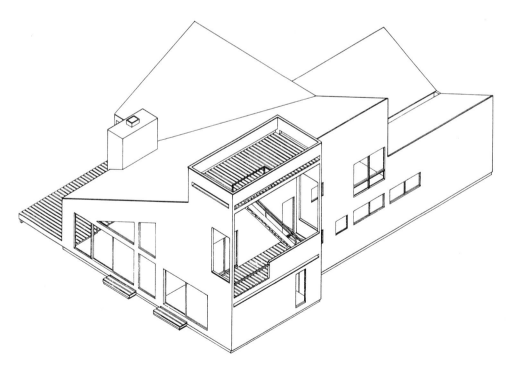

Axonometric drawing of a vacation house showing windows (fenestration, voids, cutouts) in the exterior walls (enveloping surfaces, vertical planes).

without clear boundaries, or it can be crisply defined, figural, and contained, with discernable shape and boundaries. A closet or bathroom is a space; so are the mall in Washington, D.C., and New York's Central Park.

Building components familiar to everyone are favorites for renaming. Windows become "fenestration," "voids" in walls, "oculi," "penetrations," "punched openings," "apertures," or "cutouts." Walls become vertical "planes," "membranes," "surfaces," "space definers or delimiters," "enclosing envelopes," "partitions," or "separators." A courtyard may be an "atrium," a "peristyle," or an "interior open space," whereas a porch translates into a "loggia," a "portico," or a "transitional space." Corridors are called "galleries," "circulation conduits," "pedestrian streets," "passages," "channels," "ambulatories," and, even "hallways."

Critics and students like to talk about the visual characteristics of form. Representative of some of the nouns and adjectives one hears are the following:

Scale Having to do with the relative sizes of the whole and its constituent parts, and in turn their relation to human dimensions. When architects talk about scale, they usually are concerned with design perception—about how small or large something looks within a given context because of its composition and proportions.

Appropriateness Whether a design fits or reflects the circumstances of a project. Appropriateness can relate to the scale, style, character, or functional purpose of a design.

Image The overall look and feel of a place or building.

Texture, shape, rhythm, relief, color, dimension Pseudo-objectifiable but critical visual qualities characteristic of architectural form.

Metaphor A term denoting the ability of architecture to look, be like, or represent something else—buildings as "machines," living "organisms," geometric solids (cubes, spheres, rectangular "slabs" or "bars," cylinders, lattices, pyramids, chains, mats, or combinations of these), other human-made constructions (including such things as tools, furniture, bridges, containers, musical instruments,

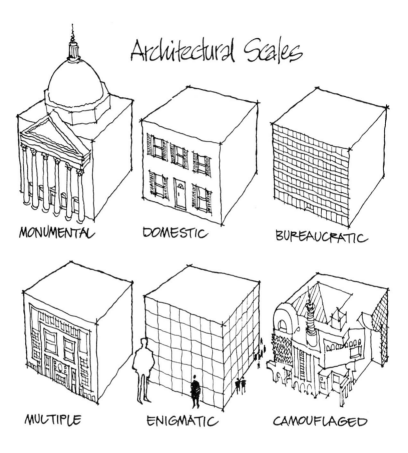

Architectural Scales

MONUMENTAL DOMESTIC BUREAUCRATIC

MULTIPLE ENIGMATIC CAMOUFLAGED

and works of art), or ideas and concepts derived from literature, religion, philosophy, science or art.

Function Refers to the role of architecture in fulfilling objectifiable human requirements relating to utility, structural stability, comfort and safety, buildability, and cost. The presumption is that functional considerations are different from aesthetic ones in that they are rational, somewhat quantifiable and measurable, and not ego-dependent.

Form, formal, formalistic Very broad terms relating to the physical, three-dimensional, distinctly visual nature and shape of those things designed or studied by architects. Objects, buildings, spaces, structural elements, ornaments, cities, and plants all have "form" and "formal/formalistic" qualities.

Typology A noun ("typological" is the adjective) borrowed from linguistics and referring to classifiable sets of objects (e.g., building types, house types, room types, street types, bridge types) that share common, identifiable patterns of structure and form, independent of their individual historical origin, style, or function.

Circulation Often-used word describing the "form," pattern, and method of movement within or through an environment—circulation of people, vehicles, and goods horizontally and vertically in buildings, cities, rooms, or landscapes. The circulation system is often the formal backbone of many building types.

Unity, harmony, coherence Denoting in any composition that quality whereby the whole and its parts appear to belong together primarily through visual linkages and perceptible interrelationships, of which there can be many (dependent on the eye of the beholder).

Disunity, incoherence, fragmentation The opposite of the preceding terms, also dependent on individual perception (one person's harmony may be another's incoherence).

Layering and layers The perception of multiple elements—walls, rows of columns or trees, doors or windows, roofs, ornamentation—distributed in space so that the observer sees several at one time proceeding from foreground to background, side to side, or top to bottom. If you look down a city street, you will see "layers" of buildings lining the street, "layers" of signs and columns and storefronts and sidewalk elements including trees, benches, parking meters.

It reads Meaning that a design intent can be seen, stands out, and can be interpreted ("read" like a book or a facial expression). Examples of "reading" buildings can include the reading of two- and three-dimensional compositional patterns, of functions within, of materials and structure, of symbolic content (think of Gothic cathedrals or the New York Stock Exchange). If a building cannot be "read," according to the critic, then the architect may need to "rewrite."

*Friedrich Schinkel's early nineteenth-century perspective draw-
ing of a theater for Berlin. Note that the building is a composition
of rectangular and cylindrical forms layered horizontally and vertically, unified by repetition of elements and continuous bands of
ornamentation, and given scale by such recognizable features
as stair risers and windows in the rusticated stone base.*

Hundreds of adjectives season the comments and critiques of architects, especially when making remarks about students' work. A few are heard often:

Interesting A word meaning anything from boring, banal, passable, or conventional to provocative, inventive, stimulating, or witty. An "interesting" design rarely merits an A, whereas "very interesting" may be in the A category.

Competent Like "interesting," may imply that a design is merely okay, workable, acceptable, but certainly not brilliant or revolutionary. Competent is what every architect is expected to be at a minimum.

Convincing Cropping up regularly, it usually means that a specific design appears to be well thought out *and* well executed in the drawings or model of the design. "Convincing" says that you have created something believable both artistically and functionally.

Ugly Yes, "ugly" is heard frequently. It really means that the critic does not like the looks of what you have designed, for whatever reasons (on which he or she may never elaborate) whereas others may instead find your design . . .

Beautiful The critic likes the looks of your design, also for reasons that may not always be clear. Remember that in architecture, like all other art, much of the perception of beauty is in the eye of the beholder.

Meaningful, meaningless Judgments about what designs "say," represent, stand for, denote, and connote, beyond what they actually do or look like. Columns, for example, are vertical structural elements that support loads and play a role in a building's composition, but they also could have additional meaning, standing for such things as virility, continuity, verticality, trees, victory, connection between heaven and earth, or any other idea advocated by their designer or supported by the scholarship of historians. For some teachers and architects, designs that cannot be thusly read or interpreted are therefore "meaningless," as sometimes may be the word "meaningful."

Throughout this book, you will encounter much more of the architect's vocabulary; this is only the proverbial tip of the iceberg.

Perhaps it is the uncertainty and subjectivity of architectural values that lead architects to search so relentlessly for a more scientific language, for a new set of words and definitions every year. And every year, with each new batch of jargon and classifiers, the vocabulary list lengthens, while the uncertainty and subjectivity persist as always. Thus, beginning architectural students should remember that this is part of the tradition and should not let first-year language shock deter the quest for creative solutions, enlightenment, and rationality.

Competition and Grades

Many who start architectural school never finish. There are many reasons that people drop out, the work load and competition being among them. However, few students quit simply because of the amount of work, to which most quickly become accustomed. On the other hand, there is a keen and discernable atmosphere of competition, intensified by the artistic nature of the work in design studio, and this atmosphere can discourage even the most hard working.

Most institutions use grades to indicate how students are doing with respect to the competition within the class or school. This is certainly not unique to architecture. What is unique is that diligence and hard work do not necessarily bring correspondingly high grades. In fact another of the great first-year shocks may occur when a project you have designed with all the blood, sweat, tears, time, and imagination you could summon gets judged a failure. And this can happen inconsistently and without warning. You may have received an A or B on your last project, then a C, D, or F on the next one. What should you make of this?

First, it is all normal. Your work, not you, is what is being judged. Most students experience the roller coaster of project grading throughout school, and it takes getting used to. Many students have both good and bad semesters, good and bad months, weeks, or days. Keep reminding yourself that effort alone is not being assessed in architecture school, that native aptitude and talent are essential and even dominant evaluation factors.

Second, most faculty grade students' work in architectural design both on a curve (that is, relative to only those students in a section or class) and against some broader set of standards applied to all students. Occasionally every project in a section falls short or, conversely, earns an A or B. Semesters occur during which no one receives an A, and others when nearly everyone receives an A. This depends on the critic—some may have unrealistically high standards—as well as the students.

You must be philosophical about grading, recognizing that grades represent only the combined objective and subjective evaluation of your work at a particular time. They may change as you proceed through school and as your work changes. They neither destroy nor ensure your future career. Once you are out of architectural school, probably no one will ever again see or care about your grades as a student. But one thing is certain: if you do not make the effort and do the work, you will not receive good grades, no matter how gifted you are.

The competition in architectural school is typical of grade competition anywhere else. Once admitted, you are expected to maintain some minimum grade point average (GPA) for continuation in the program. Most graduate schools require a minimum GPA of B (3.0) for graduation. Many programs do not allow architecture students to proceed to the next level of design studio with less than adequate performance in design, even if their GPA is high enough. Therefore students feel pressured by the need to maintain their academic standing, but this is usually a problem for a minority of students in a class.

Wanting to excel, to stand out, to be on top or at least near it, is a source of both stress and motivation. Competitive pressure is internal and external. Dedicated students push themselves, notwithstanding other influences, reacting to an internal need to achieve. With this comes pushing from external sources—faculty, fellow students, friends, and family—which can be relentless and unending. Some students thrive on such pressures; others feel substantial anxiety, which can affect their work. The pressures are there, the competition and pushing are inevitable, and you must at least cope with them. Ideally they will cause you to do your best and suc-cced, happily.

Pencilphobia

Pencil and paper are the architect's primary tools, even in the age of the computer, which is merely another form of tool for creating drawings. And drawing is the primary medium for the exploration of architectural design. Like all other artists and craftspersons, architects must thoroughly master the use of tools through practice and repetition. Good architects become so comfortable and facile with their drawing instruments that they cannot engage in the act of design except with a drawing tool—either a pencil or a mouse—in hand. In designing architecture, the mind, body, and tool merge, acting together as one. No architect can design simply by thinking and visualizing mentally.

Prior to mastering computer-aided drawing, students must learn to sketch and draft with pencil, ink, or other media. For design, such drawing entails exploring and expressing conceptual hypotheses graphically, and making proposals and decisions on paper. Some beginning architecture students discover this painfully. They develop a fear of committing themselves and their ideas to paper, a fear of drawing—albeit an unconscious fear. The reluctance to draw stems from anxiety and uncertainty. Beginning students quickly learn that without a drawing to look at, the critic assumes that there is no design yet and nothing tangible to evaluate. Many design teachers refuse to discuss students' design proposals or ideas unless they have been drawn. At the same time, students discover that teachers may make what seem to be exclusively negative comments when the indispensable drawings are presented. So it is not unusual for some students to acquire pencilphobia as a defense, a way of avoiding the risk of being criticized.

Architectural design is inherently a conjectural, trial-and-error process. Drawings are the primary means by which to hypothesize (to try) alternative designs, evaluate them, then refine and perfect

them through the discovery and purging of errors or inappropriate ideas. Design is a continuous trial-test-change process. Without this iterative struggle using pencil and paper (and often models), you will not go far as an architectural designer. Therefore draw freely, willingly, and accurately. More design study sketches are always better than fewer. Twenty minutes of thoughtful criticism, even if disapproving, is far more valuable than two minutes of verbal lamentations and regrets.

The Culture and Community of Architecture School

During your first year in architecture school, you will sense a school culture and community of which you are becoming a part. It is unique to schools of architecture, regardless of the university. The sense of culture and community exists for several reasons. Most architecture schools are small, making it easy to get to know well a large percentage of the students and faculty within a year or two. Architecture students spend enormous amounts of time working together—day and night—within the school building, especially in studios. At many schools, students spend weeks or months during summer or other semesters traveling and studying together in Europe. Groups of students frequently work on projects in local communities. All of this personal interaction promotes bonding, typically lacking among students in other academic disciplines, which is reinforced by the rigors of sharing a common mission: the challenge of mastering architecture.

Many architects look back on architecture school as one of their most formative and rewarding life experiences, a time when they not only felt intensely stimulated intellectually and creatively, but also closest to their friends and academic colleagues. Some liken it to spending several years in boot camp. Most remember the positive experiences, forgetting or suppressing memories of the more arduous or disappointing moments all students faced.

Architecture students not only bond with other students; they also may form affiliations with faculty they respect and admire, faculty with whom they study and work closely. Such bonds are usually based on some combination of personal resonance and shared academic interests. Students usually are drawn to mentors with whom they feel comfortable intellectually and personally, who show concern for their work, or who are close in age. Teachers vary tremendously in comportment and teaching style, and this affects how students relate to them. Some are aloof and distant, while others seem easygoing and approachable. Students may never get to know some teachers well, while others could be best buddies. Of course, what matters most is how effectively teachers teach—how well they help students realize their potential in the field of architecture.

Despite all the bonding and shared experiences in architecture school, social structures nevertheless appear. Students inevitably make special friends and form groups. Motivated by mutual personal or academic interests, or by similar social, cultural, and ethnic backgrounds, students naturally seek out and affiliate with those students with whom they feel comfortable. Consequently, subgroups of students tend to stick together because they are: especially artistic or intellectual; Hispanic, Asian American, or African American; foreign or female; older or married; fraternity members or sports enthusiasts.

Another structure or hierarchy may exist in many schools. Design is academically the core of architectural education, the curricular endeavor for which native talent is indispensable. Therefore students who excel in design inadvertently acquire a certain status in the eyes of both students and faculty. They are the "gifted" ones who set the standards of performance in the design studio. This status may manifest itself subtly, but it also can be acknowledged quite overtly. Top design students may get extra attention and even deference from design critics; more respected and willingly indulged by critics, they may be able to break the project rules—which other students feel obliged to follow—with greater impunity; they are more frequently asked for crits by other students; and, naturally, they receive more jury praise. Such status is problematic only to the extent that it is perceived to be undeserved or that it results in other students' being shortchanged, especially students who excel in areas other than design. But it is simply a fact of life in architecture school: design talent and performance are the most valued assets.

The Jury System

No other tradition in architectural school is as tenacious and enduring as the jury review. The jury review marks the end of work on a design project, or project phase, when students present their presumably finished drawings and models for evaluation by an assembled group of critics, the esteemed jury. Juries are typically composed of the studio critic, other invited faculty, and outside guests who may be architects or hypothetical clients. The jury review is considered a significant component of the architect's educational experience, so it is almost always a public event, with students, including students from other studio classes, attending from beginning to end.

The typical review involves students' hanging their work on the wall and, in turn, standing in front of their drawings and models, all eyes upon them, while making an oral presentation of their project to the jury. Often the graphic presentation speaks for itself, but the student nevertheless is expected to advocate his or her concept verbally and subsequently to engage in dialogue with members of the jury following the initial presentation. This seems straightforward enough, but in fact it is not an educational experience familiar to most students prior to arriving in architectural school. Thus to appreciate the jury experience, consider these specific observations.

You must first imagine yourself as the student preparing for the jury. Two concerns preoccupy your every waking moment: (1) Will you have a complete presentation with drawings and models both comprehensible and finished? (2) Will your design be praised or ridiculed by the jury? Although these are separate concerns, they are nevertheless related.

Satisfactorily completing work and meeting deadlines depend on the ability to manage time, organize tasks, make decisions, and draw. You quickly learn in the first year of school that it is a sin to pin up an incomplete presentation for the jury to scrutinize. The jurors, usually three or more in number, will almost always cite students whose work is unfinished, vaguely described, or unreadable, regardless of the merits of the students' creative or conceptual thinking. Sometimes jurors refuse to review incomplete presentations, especially if the student attempts to fill in the gaps verbally. Typically jurors chastise the beleaguered student, expressing dismay, disappointment, or even anger.

Jurors who believe in positive reinforcement might say: "This could have been a great scheme, if only we could have seen all of it," or "One more week and this could have been fully and very successfully developed," or "It's a shame that your presentation doesn't do justice to your idea," or "What we see only suggests its potential quality."

Jurors believing in negative reinforcement might say: "You certainly had enough time to finish this project," or "How can you ask us to review so flimsy a presentation?" or "You're never going to make it with presentations like this," or "Why do you expect us to waste our time on incomplete work?" or "The least we expect is completion of the *minimum* required drawings."

Often jurors lace their remarks with humor and sympathy, but just as often with sarcasm and disdain. In anticipation or even fear of being on the receiving end of such attacks, students mount heroic efforts to be or appear to be complete when the deadline arrives. But students vary considerably in their ability to pace themselves, budget time, and produce drawings and models. Some, quick to make decisions and skillful in drawing, finish with relative ease, while others struggle to finish.

The other preoccupation before each jury concerns the project itself. Will the proposed design be marginally acceptable? competent? perhaps good? maybe even outstanding? Since the question of quality is one of judgment in the eyes of the jurors, it is a relative preoccupation. You may love your design, and your design critic may love it, but the jury might not.

Anticipating a jury's response to a project is impossible. Further, anxiety about the jury's response is intensified because of the tremendous investment of effort, thought, and creative energy made prior to the jury. You say to yourself, "That's not just my work hanging up there. That's me!" Consequently, you interpret a criticism of your design as a criticism of you personally. Either consciously or subconsciously, you think, "If they don't like my work, then they don't like *me!*"

Telling you that this is not true—that jurors are evaluating your work, not you as a person—is no guarantee that such feelings will disappear. You know that you will feel good if the jury seems to like your work and bad if they do not — hence the anxiety.

Another factor contributes to jury jitters for many students: the jury limelight, the public nature of it all. There they are, faculty and students, professionals and peers, staring at you and your presentation, waiting to see if you succeed or fail. The blood rushes, palms sweat, mouth dries, the words you intended pronouncing never come forth. You worry about appearing foolish, showing anger or embarrassment, fumbling with your notes, perhaps even shedding tears, arguing insultingly with a juror who has maligned your efforts. For some students, mundane and insignificant preoccupations may intrude upon consciousness under the pressure of standing before a jury, life on the line. "How do I look? fly open? Do I smell?" After a charrette, these concerns may be justifiable.

For many students, anticipating the jury review is exhilarating. It is a kind of show and tell, sometimes a game of one-upmanship. Such students are usually self-confident, no matter what the quality of their work, and they relish the challenge of the jury review and the opportunity to show their stuff. It can be an ego trip if you believe in yourself and your work, even in the face of negative criticism. Those with gambling or risk-taking instincts welcome the unpredictability of the jury, hoping to win while knowing that there is always a chance of losing.

No description of the jury system would be complete without portraying the behavioral characteristics of jurors: what they do and say and how they interact with students and with each other. Assessing architectural design is in part a subjective, taste-dependent process, so each juror brings to the review his or her own particular agenda—a collection of interests, opinions, prejudices, and idiosyncrasies. Students in a jury commonly hear remarks made by jurors that seem vague, unclear, confusing, contradictory, needlessly deprecating, self-laudatory, or irrelevant. Especially amusing, though sometimes confusing to the student being reviewed, can be debates between jurors. The debate may begin over the student's work, but frequently it progresses into a more general disagreement over opposing polemics or conflicting values. Such debates can also be

very enlightening to those students awake and listening, for the arguments always apply to projects other than the one on the wall.

Some jurors are relatively silent and passive, saving their remarks for propitious moments, or they comment on only the weightiest of issues. Jurors intimidate each other, depending on interpersonal chemistry. Some are very talkative and demonstrative, seizing every opening to take the floor. Others pontificate about the world of architecture and the human condition. Jurors may say little that is specific about the work on the wall, or they may offer detailed, specific criticism of the student's design.

Some jurors dominate the jury owing to their verbal wit, voluminous memory and powers of recall, professional prominence, personal charisma, or persistent intervention. Still others specialize, talking about only about one aspect of architectural design—site planning, structure, energy conservation, formal composition—to the exclusion of other aspects. Eventually students get to know the faculty well enough to predict what they will focus on, although they can rarely predict their reactions.

After the review—hearing both praise and criticism at the same time, hearing that this is good while that is bad—students may not know whether the jurors approved or disapproved, whether the jury comments were positive or negative. The students wonder what silence on the part of a juror means, and they cringe whenever the word "but . . ." rings out. Some jurors sketch directly on students' drawings to make their point or illustrate an idea. If they are thoughtful, they do it in pencil, although sketches in ink or colored marker may make a more indelible impression. Students strain to interpret jurors' implicit reactions: their demeanor, facial expressions, body movements, and inaudible utterances. Jurors cover their mouths and chins, scratch their heads or cheeks, lean precariously forward in their chairs, get up and walk around while studiously eyeing the drawings or model. They continually whisper to one another or pass notes. What are they thinking? Is it plus or minus?

The confusion may be compounded when, hours or days after the jury, the student learns from his or her studio critic that the jurors thought highly of the project, whereas the student's impression was the opposite. Having believed the jury review a disaster and feeling discouraged, the student is pleasantly surprised when the studio critic conveys the good news. But the opposite occurs. The student senses that the jury went well, or remembers only positive comments, and then, after the ensuing period of elation and pride, learns that the jurors thought the work, on the whole, quite mediocre. Of course individual jurors do not always agree as to the quality of student work, and it is not unusual to receive an A or B from one while another dispenses a C or D. However, most jury grades cluster. Ultimately, the studio critic is responsible for the grade, reporting it to the student either verbally or in writing.

Some architectural students and teachers question the value of the traditional jury as a pedagogical technique. They argue that it is excessively time-consuming—juries can easily last five or six hours, depending on the size of the class and number of jurors (more jurors means more time)—and too frequently degrading to students. They claim that juries are repetitious, with the same comments heard over and over again. To them, juries are boring, destructive, self-indulgent word games for faculty that serve only to put down the students. Also some argue that the jury process places undue emphasis on presentation graphics at the expense of design content and conceptual quality.

Although some criticisms are well founded, the jury system nevertheless survives because it accomplishes goals otherwise impossible to achieve: it simulates to some extent the reality of making presentations in practice; it reinforces the importance of meeting deadlines; it provides a forum for students to see each other's work and for faculty to see the work of students other than their own; and it encourages and reinforces development of both graphic and oral presentation skills. Most important, the intellectual discourse during a lively and thoughtful jury review is as valuable for students as any lecture or seminar. Insightful jurors pose vital and probing questions, challenge conventional thinking and assumptions, raise issues perhaps overlooked, and stimulate new thinking. Jury discussions can surprise not only the studio students but also the studio critic.

Like it or not, the architectural jury, which represents one of the unique, recurring experiences in architectural education, is here to stay. It is, after all, the ceremonial culmination of each studio design project, the place where all of the skills, knowledge, and ideas of the prospective architect must fuse and find expression. In judging design, it celebrates design and the art of architecture.

Other Traditions

As you might guess from reading about studio courses and juries, design activity dominates other course work and activities in most architectural schools. At times the demands of the studio, coupled with poor time management by students, totally eclipse the performance of other academic duties. Teachers of history or technology courses can count on extensive absenteeism just prior to scheduled design studio deadlines and juries, particularly at the end of each semester. Or they know that, during charrettes, students attending their classes will either sleep or sit as if in a state of semiconsciousness, eyes open, breathing slowed, swaying back and forth almost imperceptibly in their chairs, hearing and absorbing practically nothing. Occasionally, after extensive sleep deprivation, students may get a second wind that keeps them momentarily alert, but this is unusual.

Students also learn to capitalize on scheduling conflicts between courses. A favorite ploy is to explain to your studio critic that you are behind in design, normally evidenced by a lack of drawings, because you had to study for a structures exam or write a history paper. You beg for understanding and compassion for your deficiencies in structures or history because you had to meet a design studio deadline and have not slept for three days. Most students, when faced with the choice, give first priority to design, knowing that the final jury review is pending and assuming that they can somehow catch up on assignments or exams in their other courses. Unfortunately, if too much is postponed, they may not catch up until subsequent semesters.

Communal spirit is infectious in architectural school, even with the extreme competition and pressure, and faculty and students seem to find ways to enjoy themselves regularly and share their interests and sense of common purpose. Typical of the events that reinforce this communality are informal weekly get-togethers in schools featuring wine and cheese, beer and pretzels, lectures or group discussions, slide presentations or other such diversions. Field trips and travel expeditions are frequently organized, sometimes to faraway and exotic places during summer, Christmas, or spring vacations. Students and faculty often get together socially in small groups or by class, and the conversation usually involves a lot of shop as well as small talk.

Some schools have annual "beaux arts balls," another tradition borrowed from Paris. Usually planned by students, they are typically costume and theme parties emulating great European balls of times past. They are characterized by incredibly inventive, outrageous costumes, loud and raucous music, extravagant decorations, generous supplies of food and drink, and sometimes questionable behavior. Balls are held in both school buildings and off campus. Do not assume, however, that all architectural schools sponsor beaux arts balls. With or without them, there are always plenty of student-sponsored parties, sometimes after juries are over, to release tensions.

One of the more lamentable traditions in architectural school is periodic burnout. Perhaps this should be called a behavior pattern rather than a tradition. Its symptoms are reduced motivation, loss of interest and morale, lack of zeal and commitment, and an overwhelming desire either to drop out or to just graduate and move on. Some years burnout may seem to run rampant, like a plague, whereas in other years, it occurs rarely.

To fathom this phenomenon, recall the intensity and pace of work in the first one or two years in architectural school, when the learning curve is steepest and, for most students, morale and educational gratification run high. Regardless of what occurs in subsequent years, it is difficult for any program to sustain the energy and rate of discovery experienced in the beginning years. Even the trials and tribulations described earlier contribute to the exhilaration and peer-group coherence of the initial year or two. But things change, and later burnout is attributable to several of these changes.

First, attrition and dropping out may affect students in a class, especially when friends or talented colleagues disappear. Second, some of the mystery of architecture and design vanishes, making the process seem somehow less intriguing or challenging than before. Third, work is done with increasing independence on the part of students and decreasing intervention by teachers, and some students miss the boot camp, basic training unity of the beginning year or two. Indeed some may miss it because they are unable to perform well without it. Fourth, students may begin feeling that architecture is not for them, that it is too competitive or unrewarding. If they are not excelling, they may be disappointed in themselves and unwilling to be second best. Finally, they may genuinely lose interest while finding new interests, being distracted by economic or romantic temptations.

All of these changes can produce the same effect: poorer work, cynicism, boredom, and, in some cases, the abandonment of architecture, either temporarily or permanently. The concentration demanded by architectural work makes success elusive when there are competing distractions or obligations. Even talented students take leaves of absence or postpone taking courses when circumstances outside school inhibit their in-school performance.

Thus related to the burnout tradition is the tradition of postponement, temporary dropping out, or deferral of course work, particularly in design. This is not necessarily a bad tradition. There is no negative stigma associated with taking extra time to finish architectural school, and it is often advisable for many students. Many successful architects had educations that required a few more semesters than originally anticipated.

For economic reasons many architectural students feel compelled to hold jobs while they go through school. They may work for architects, but some do other kinds of work unrelated or marginally related to architecture. If such work consumes a reasonable amount of time in relation to the student's academic load, employment poses no problem. For example, students carrying a full academic schedule—fourteen to seventeen credit hours per term—can comfortably work eight to ten hours per week without jeopardizing their schoolwork.

But students who try to work half-time (twenty hours per week) or more while trying to perform successfully as full-time architecture students are unlikely to do well. Many attempt it; few succeed, because the effort demanded in school, especially by the design studio, will conflict with job demands. And time and energy expended on a job will detract from the quality of work in school.

In the long run it is better to forgo those extra weekly hours in a job, even at the cost of incurring debt, than to compromise the quality of one's professional education.

The traditions mentioned here are all part of the architectural school experience, but the experience cannot be fully appreciated without some understanding of those who teach architecture. So read on, for it is the professors—and what they profess—who kindle the fires of learning.

5

Professors and What They Profess

The faculty is by far the most critical factor affecting the direction and quality of any architecture school. A school's physical facilities and resources, location, and size are considerations, but they matter much less than the professors and what they profess. Architecture schools attract a variety of individual personalities, most of whom love teaching and the stimulation of an academic environment, and many of whom you will not forget, long after finishing school. Following are some insights into the nature of teachers of architecture, into how and what they teach.

The Professors

Scholars

In architectural school, traditional scholars for the most part are historians. Their work, outside of teaching classes, is focused on research, writing books and articles for scholarly journals, lecturing, and attending conferences with other like-minded scholars. Their work might focus on specific periods and places, stylistic movements of the past, or individual architects whose work may or may not be well known. They usually have good memories for names and dates, and both their speaking and writing are amply footnoted.

Designer/Practitioners

> These men and women practice architecture and teach design studio as well. Their time is usually split between office and school, serving both clients and students, and their teaching is greatly influenced by their practice. They tend to be pragmatic and idealistic at the same time, concerned with the act of building as well as the art of design. To students, design teachers who practice generally represent real-world points of view and ideologies. Often their work influences the work of their students. But their work may also be viewed with some disdain by designers who are theoreticians.

Designer/Theoreticians

> Many of these teachers engage in little or no practice, and never in conventional practice. Their claim to fame lies in professing theories of design, both in class and through writings and lectures. Since many designer/theoreticians advocate specific philosophies and design formulas, they readily attract to their studio courses students in need of an aesthetic and methodological compass. Designer/theoreticians generally give studio problems focused more on formal and less on functional, social, or technological issues.

Student Advocates

> All schools have faculty who identify or hang out with students, who empathize and communicate with them almost as peers. They may be close in age to the students or may share their point of view. Student advocate faculty types may spend a lot of time at the school, and they act as sounding boards for students' grievances. Their behavior may aggravate or provoke mixed feelings (of disapproval and guilt) in faculty who do not share their advocacy or rapport with students.

Student Adversaries

> The advocate's opposite, the student adversary is frequently critical of or at odds with students in the school. Students may perceive such faculty as acting distrustfully, disrespectfully, and disinterestedly toward them, as being unsympathetic, excessively demanding, or abrasive. Such faculty may seem to lack a sense of

humor, making them even more inscrutable. But they may well be among the most effective teachers and, in their own way, be upholding the students' best interests.

Young (or Old) Turks

Some faculty members habitually encourage reform or revolution, continually challenging the status quo. They may disregard rules and conventions for the sake of a cause, making a point of their nonconformity—sometimes subtly, sometimes with great fanfare. Often they are perceived by students as advocates. Young Turks are not necessarily radicals or anarchists, tendencies clearly discouraged in the halls of academe. To those who resist change or challenge, they are like tiny stones lodged in one's shoes: they do not prevent walking, but their presence is always felt.

Good Ol' Boys

This subgroup of faculty usually has seniority and enjoys telling stories of "how it used to be." Some may be burned out as teachers, having run out of ideas or become bored with teaching the same course year after year. Others may help set the tone of the school and influence school policy and management. They may be prone to share gossip, shop talk, and rounds of drinks. Old boys in a school may symbolize permanence and continuity to some, decadence and atrophy to others. Rarely are there any good ol' girls in this group, but this may change as more women join faculties.

Logicians

Logicians circumvent the uncertainty and subjectivity of architectural design. They have little patience for inconclusive discussions of aesthetics. For them, most phenomena are explainable, subject at all times to rational powers of analysis. They usually adopt the approach of the scientist or engineer while merely tolerating that of the artist. They arm themselves well with data and methodology.

Obfuscators

A few teachers employ vocabularies and manners of expression unintelligible to most students. They are hard to understand and tedious to listen to, notwithstanding the significance or depth of

what they have to say. Obfuscators, not satisfied with simple, straightforward language, seek richness and complexity in the use of English and equivalent richness and complexity in the thinking that produced the English. Unfortunately this correlation may not always occur. Related to the obfuscator are the mumbler and the "um-um-um-umer." They also have speaking habits that many students find obstructive to listening and learning.

Zealous Administrators

Running every school is a chair or dean, along with appropriate deputies (titled associate, assistant, or something else). Many of these are intensely involved in leading and managing the school, and their zeal carries over into all parts of the program, providing inspiration to faculty and students. But excessive zeal can be obstructive, patronizing, or misdirected. From the students' point of view, the best administrator is one whose zeal is directed toward advocating and protecting student interests. From the teachers' point of view, the ideal administrator does the same for the faculty while ensuring smooth and efficient departmental operations.

Laid-back Administrators

The opposite of the zealous administrator, this type of administrator pursues a laissez-faire policy of management and leadership. He or she assumes that faculty are best left free to stoke their own furnaces, to identify and develop their own interests, and to set their own standards. Laid-back administrators may be active in the life of the school while nevertheless maintaining low profiles. They often delegate much of the administrative work to assistants, secretaries, committees, and individual faculty members.

Separatists

The separatist is a faculty member who has rejected the "if you can't lick 'em, then join 'em" philosophy and instead embraced the "if you can't lick 'em, then leave 'em" philosophy regarding intrafaculty relationships. Not surprisingly, many architectural schools have faculty who, for various reasons, cannot get along with one or several other faculty. Or there may be a small group or faction that finds itself at odds with other factions. To cope with this situation, separatists may simply avoid those colleagues with whom there is conflict. The source of conflict and tension may be ideological or political, and is usually related to academic issues. Teachers may disagree about architectural style, methods of instruction, course content, administrative policy, or curricular direction. Being frequently unaccommodating and obstinate in their positions, if not dogmatic and unreasonable, they choose to retreat from the battlefront in order to safeguard their domain of opinion. Some never leave it.

Inscrutables

There are always a few silent types teaching architecture, individuals who appear introverted and shy. These characteristics may be less apparent in the classroom or in the company of close companions. Inscrutable ones are sometimes hard to get to know, for both students and faculty, since they tend to reveal their thoughts and feelings quite sparingly, seldom lowering their guard or exposing themselves emotionally. Inscrutability can be a defense or a wise offense when silence is appropriate or needed.

Venerable Heroes

In many schools there is often a faculty member, either permanent or visiting, whose fame and prestige are such that he or she inspires adulation, emulation, and respect. These heroes may be famous because of their work as designers, historians, or theoreticians. They may be seen as great innovators or trendsetters, rebels or reformers. Whatever their claim to fame, they tread the halls of academe as special citizens. Students await their every utterance with great anticipation, hoping that it will be of profound significance. No one contradicts or challenges them except with the utmost politeness and diplomacy. They can be idols in architectural education—until they lose their edge or fall out of fashion.

Some -Isms and -Ologies

Listen long enough to any faculty member at any school of architecture, and you will be able eventually to identify what he or she is advocating or professing. I refer here not to the specific subject matter they teach but rather to the more general philosophy, cause, or movement to which they subscribe, no matter what courses they are responsible for.

Any teacher offering instruction in a given subject, such as architectural history or design, inevitably brings to the subject his or her own beliefs and values about the world—about culture, religion, social behavior, politics, economics, and aesthetics. For some, this set of beliefs may be organized into a formalized, personal ideology or philosophy that continually influences opinions and actions, including what is conveyed to students in the classroom. Even teaching a subject that appears to be value free and nonideological, such as structural analysis, drawing, or physics, may be accompanied

by subtle expressions of the teacher's beliefs and philosophy. Course readings, subtopics, and organization imply a network of values advocated by the teacher. Thus teachers can be very powerful, transmitting much more than information and techniques.

Architects and architectural educators cultivate such philosophies because a designer cannot make good architecture without taking a theoretical or philosophical position about architecture. This is

one attribute of architecture that differentiates it so notably from engineering or other fields in which most decisions are based on commonly accepted scientific principles, data, and methodological protocols.

Consider engineering. After sufficiently defining the problem to be solved (ventilate a space or make a faster microprocessor, for example), an engineer sets about designing a system to solve the stated problem most efficiently. Design efficiency is measured by applying specific evaluation criteria such as least cost, highest yield, least weight, greatest speed or strength, fewest number of parts, or easiest fabrication. Some judgment enters into the selection and weighting of criteria, since engineering design requires trade-offs between conflicting advantages and disadvantages. But most engineering decisions are made objectively and dispassionately, with designs tested through performance. And the engineer does not depend on some personal design philosophy to solve the engineering problem successfully.

The architect, like the engineer, may try to "optimize" building performance, as if buildings could be solutions to well-defined problems. But architecture, being more than engineered construction, is an ill-defined problem. For any given site, client, and functional program, there can be countless numbers of acceptable problem-solving designs that can meet performance requirements. Indeed, no matter how precisely one defines the design problem, there always will be an array of design possibilities and variations worth considering. How, then, does the architectural designer decide which option to choose? Making these choices is the art, rather than the science, of architecture—the aspect of design that demands more than engineering methods.

The built environment provides shelter and space for human activity, but architecture also affects our feelings and emotions, engaging both our senses and intellect. The ancient Roman architect Vitruvius, considered Western civilization's first architectural theorist, wrote that good architecture offers commodity, firmness, *and* delight. Thus architecture has long been seen, thought of, and taught as a form of expressive art for which generative aesthetic philosophies and theories are needed to justify design choices (when objective evaluation criteria are absent) or to uncover and explain architectural meanings. Today, therefore, the challenge of teaching and learning design stems from the vast assortment of available philosophies and theories, none of which can be demonstrated to be right or wrong with conclusive proof. Similarly, the challenge continues into architectural practice, where the nascent designer must apply his or her evolving philosophy.

What, then, are some of the -isms and -ologies—those beliefs and values affecting architectural education and practice—professed by architecture school faculty? Most pedagogical philosophies relate to one or more of the following:

Formal composition, morphology

History, historicism, and historic preservation

Science and engineering, technology

Deconstructivism

Human behavior, sociology, and psychology

The natural environment, ecology

The urban environment, urbanism

Symbolism

Mysticism, theology

Pragmatism, functionalism

Capitalism, socialism, fascism, communism

The items listed cover a multitude of ideas, many overlapping. However, they help organize the ensuing discussion of what professors espouse in the cause of architecture.

Morphology

In biology the study of the form and shape of organisms is called *morphology*. An organism is, by definition, a whole and complete thing or biological system, something contained and circumscribed. In architecture, by analogy, we talk of morphology with respect to building form. Unlike natural organisms, architecture is human-made and takes its form, in part, through an act of will of the designer. Although there can be many forces acting on the designer and the design, they nevertheless may be insufficient to generate an inevitable, natural form that all would agree is the "right" form. The willful act then becomes indispensable, and it is at this point that the designer turns to a philosophy or theory of architectural morphology.

Morphologists employ geometries and patterns to create a sense of order, to organize and regulate the spaces, structures, surfaces, and volumes of buildings. These regulating geometries and patterns serve to unify often complex buildings into organic wholes—to make parts of buildings seem to belong together compositionally. The sources of such geometries or patterns may be quite arbitrary, or they may be based on a convenient structural module or repeated dimension, a system of proportion, preexisting site geometries and patterns, idealized mathematical relationships not readily perceived, and so on.

Examples of the morphologist's philosophy in action are in great supply. The plans and facades of villas designed by the sixteenth-century architect Andrea Palladio, which have greatly influenced domestic Western architecture, exemplify the use of mathematical proportioning to achieve harmony and visual interrelationships between building volumes, rooms, exterior walls, and details. Ratios established between widths, lengths, and heights of elements—rooms, courts, facades, and components of facades (such as columns, pilasters, and pediments)—permeate the entire design. Often architects of the Renaissance, and Roman builders before them, developed elaborate systems of proportioning derived from musical harmony ratios in the belief that such ratios were natural, and what was natural for the ear must be natural for the eye.

The use of site and floor plan grids represents another common strategy of morphological organization. Taken to its extreme in the twentieth-century office building, this method of planning can be found throughout history: in the layout of towns and cities, Roman camps, early Christian churches, and mosques built throughout the Islamic world. Some grids are not rectangular. Grid networks can be based on triangles, hexagons, and even circles. The East Building of the National Gallery of Art in Washington, D.C., designed by I. M. Pei, is composed throughout using a planning grid of triangles.

Akin to grid-based design is axis-based design. The underlying philosophy of graphic organization is to create one or more axes about which a composition is centered or arranged, often with observable symmetry and balance of elements found on opposing sides of the axes. Ideally the ends of the axes are marked by appropriate focal elements visually terminating the axes, elements such as building entrances, porticoes, towers, sculptures, gates, or gazebos. But where there is axial symmetry, there also can be axial asymmetry. Thomas Jefferson's design of the campus and rotunda

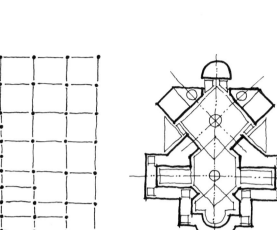

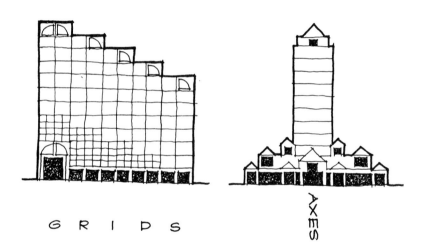

G R I D S   A X E S

at the University of Virginia illustrates well the use of symmetrical axiality as a philosophy of design. Le Corbusier's design for the government center at Chandigarh, India, illustrates asymmetrical axiality. Chandigarh's individual buildings illustrate how Le Corbusier used mixtures of grids, proportioning systems, rhythm, and repetition to generate plans and elevations.

The Chandigarh buildings reveal still another philosophical tenet important to many designers: the virtue of the recognizable geometrical solid in the architect's kit of parts. Cubes, pyramids, cylinders, and spheres are considered the most basic, irreducible

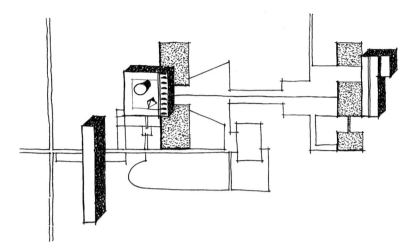

*The site plan (from left to right, the Secretariat, the Assembly
Building, and the High Court) of Chandigarh, India.*

building blocks. These "ideal," or Platonic, volumes are universally understood and recognized, are mathematically and precisely
describable, and can be combined with one another or repeated in
an infinite number of ways—cutting parts of them away, perforat-
ing them, slicing them open, fusing them together, stretching or
distorting them. Yet this design philosophy is not inevitable; it cannot be proved right or perfect. It is simply another compositional
tactic for devising formal constructions.

Historicism

Architectural history has always been a source of design inspiration
for architects, students, and teachers. The past teaches us not only
what has occurred but also what might occur, or recur, in the future
of architecture. There are different ways to react to history in making architecture. One is to extract conceptual lessons, transcending
specific periods or places, so that lessons learned may be readily
applied when and where appropriate today. For example, a morphologist might admire Palladio's exploitation of juxtaposed, solid
volumes and do the same in a contemporary structure, but without
attempting to replicate Palladio's work technically or stylistically.

Another response is to treat history as the literal, or near-literal, model for contemporary design, to assume that architects of the past have already designed and built suitable and sufficient prototypes for today's world, and that all we need do is update the models. Hardly a century has passed during the previous twenty without a period of historicism in architecture, when architects looked back admiringly at their predecessors and emulated or reproduced their predecessors' work. Motivated by nostalgia, disillusionment, or genuine adoration for bygone styles, architects periodically turn back the clock.

The philosophy of historicism, like that of the morphologist, is ultimately subjective. It reflects taste, or sometimes the lack of it. It can be faddish and transitory, inappropriate and dysfunctional, inefficient and costly. But where an act of will is needed, it provides guidance and resolution. Think about the periods and styles of architectural revival, based primarily on surficial attributes of decoration and ornamentation: Gothic, Greek, Roman, Renaissance, colonial, neoclassical, postmodern. Think of all the wonderful places and cultures offering models: Italy, France, Germany, Holland, England, Spain.

Historicist philosophy suggests that rather than trying to invent new architectural forms, we should adopt *and* adapt the forms, building traditions, and perhaps even attitudes of the past. It says that current design may replicate buildings of the past (literal adoption). Or current designs may borrow buildings, or pieces of buildings, from the past and, through distortion or graphic transformation, adapt them for new uses and buildings.

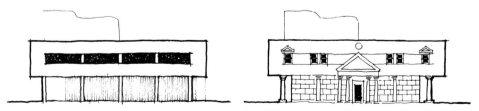

On the left, Corbusier's Villa Savoye, exemplifying the modernist, international style; on the right, the villa transformed by use of historicist decorative motifs.

Although architects have perpetually vacillated about the role of history, sometimes repeating it, sometimes adding new elements to it, the American public has always been fundamentally historicist in its design taste. American homes, furniture, building decoration, housewares, and textiles are overwhelmingly traditional in style, that is to say, historicist. We harbor some sort of tenacious, untutored reverence for an idealized past, much of which was not even ours. So-called modern design has never been popular or widely accepted, except for machines (airplanes, autos, computers, appliances, stereos). And many machines are housed in historicist packages or festooned with historicist ornamentation.

It is not uncommon to find historicists and antihistoricists among architectural school faculty. The former avow the validity and universality of historical precedent, encouraging students to look to the past for design solutions and stylistic motifs transferable to the present. The latter advocate the study of history as a source for concepts and principles, seeking to understand building typologies and styles as products of specific historical pressures incomparable to the pressures of the present. They scrutinize history, but their aim is to search continually for new forms of architectural expression without literally reproducing forms that, to them, belong to a different age.

Although labels are often misleading and simplistic, they can help readers sort out these positions. The historicist philosophy may be equated with postmodernism, while modernism is equated with antihistoricist philosophy. Most twentieth-century "modern" architects hesitate or refuse to incorporate historical motifs, styles, or vocabulary (such as Doric columns) in new buildings. Their argument (or philosophy) holds that (1) such elements are useless and costly, (2) we do not build today as we did in the past, (3) historicist or revivalist buildings are basically phony, impure, and contrived, (4) such designs are an insult and affront to buildings and architects of the past, and (5) historicism as a design philosophy is a cop-out, a refusal to confront the demands and creative opportunities of the present and future.

The historicists rebut, sometimes with much greater voice. They assert that like the American household, buildings want to be historically reverential and referential, to remind us of other times and places. Abstract, morphologically driven design is for them not enough if it ignores the past. Modern buildings seem "meaningless"—too pure, too slick, too impersonal, too denuded of familiar, comfortable details. They like moldings and cornices, pediments and double-hung windows, fluted columns and Corinthian capitals. Above all, they argue, historicism responds to a need in people—not just architects—to embrace and ensure the continuation of cultural traditions.

Not every architect or teacher is either a modernist or postmodernist, historicist or antihistoricist. Many shun such camps and labels, recognizing that reality is too complex for constraining labels and narrow philosophies.

Historic Preservation

Historic preservation is not really a design philosophy, but preservation sensibility has greatly increased throughout the world, with ever greater numbers of architects and citizens considering themselves preservationists. The preservation movement arose out of the debris left by bulldozers tearing down irreplaceable historic buildings and pieces of cities thirty years ago in the name of urban renewal. Today the desirability of preserving significant old buildings or neighborhoods is almost taken for granted. People recognize that such structures often embody substantial political, cultural, commercial, or aesthetic significance. Integral to our architectural history and cultural heritage, historic buildings also can have great economic value for their owners and their communities.

Preservation of an old building may lead either to restoration of the building's original appearance and use, or to its adaptation for new uses within its preserved exterior shell. Jefferson's Monticello and Mount Vernon, where George Washington lived, are preserved historic buildings restored to their original condition. By contrast, Boston's Quincy Market is a preserved structure adapted for new commercial uses. Sometimes older buildings are preserved, either whole or in part (often facade only), and incorporated into new construction that abuts or envelops them.

Unfortunately architectural preservationists can sometimes get carried away in their zealous attempts to save anything that is old, regardless of its age, physical condition, historic significance, or aesthetic merit. This is a percentage strategy—try to save everything and hope to save half. But misguided preservation can be unrealistic and burdensome for owners and communities, since many old buildings do not merit saving or cannot be saved at reasonable cost. Therefore architects, building owners, citizens, and public officials must exercise balanced judgment, preserving or demolishing on the basis of informed historic, technical, and financial appraisals.

Technology

The technologies of construction always have fascinated architects. The engineer in us, stimulated intellectually and manually by the workings of things mechanical and constructed, likes figuring them out. But technology has also been a source of aesthetic inspiration and invention for architects, not just an end in itself or a means to an end. For them technology can generate architectural art as much as any other generative theory.

Architects who profess and practice the art of technology are not engineers. Many approach design intuitively and qualitatively, avoiding computational involvement, which they leave to the engineers. Yet they are moved by the craft and precision, the quality and interplay of materials, the visually elegant or complex details that reflect the application of building technology.

Construction technology can be classified into various systems, including the following:

Structural systems—system elements, details of assembly

Systems of enclosure—roofing, walls, insulation, waterproofing

Thermal control—heating, cooling, ventilation

Solar energy control

Illumination—daylight, electrical

Acoustics

Systems of conveyance—stairs, elevators, escalators, ramps, conveyors

Plumbing systems—distribution of fluids and gases

Electrical distribution systems

Electronic and digital communication systems

Systems of furnishing for occupancy

Associated with all these technologies are specific materials and physical components that can be manipulated by designers, both to provide the intended technical service and to achieve willfully created artistic effects.

The designer can exploit technology as a means to architecture in many ways. Most obvious is visually expressing selected technical components: for example, the structure, structural connections, ductwork and plumbing, stairways and ramps. This design philosophy exposes and displays the guts of buildings as an aesthetic strategy, sometimes using color to heighten the observer's awareness of the exhibited components. This strategy may even save money if it avoids the expense of concealing and finishing.

A related design philosophy configures an entire building so that its overall form reflects its method of construction, its structure, and its systems of environmental control. Instead of creating a building with finishes that conceal how it was built, the designer can let the building's massing and skin reveal the elements used to construct and organize the interior. A Gothic cathedral and an Indian teepee are buildings of this kind. Many modern commercial

buildings also exemplify this philosophy: continuous vertical tubes comprising elevators, stairs, ducts, and structural elements (mostly columns) supporting layer after layer of identical floor-ceiling "sandwiches," with interior space enveloped by a "skin," a "curtain" wall literally hung on the structure.

Technology can occasionally get out of hand if architects treat buildings only as machines. If the technological bias is not offset by other biases, such machines can fail to respond to human needs omitted in the technical specifications and list of functional goals. Sometimes designers or engineers see buildings only as giant systems, skeletons, networks of ducts and pipes, or beehives of spaces laced with threads of electrical conduits. Most good architecture transcends such a singular interpretation of how or why it was created.

Deconstructivism

In the 1980s, a new and controversial architectural theory appeared and gained a foothold in the halls of academe, as well as in the profession and the media. Borrowing liberally from the field of literary criticism and the esoteric writings of French and German philosophers, a small number of architect/theoreticians—teachers and practitioners—began suggesting that buildings could and should be "deconstructed." The "decon" thesis is not an easy one to grasp. It proceeds from the fundamental premise that the perceived substance and meaning of any work of art depends as much on the observer's point of view and circumstances as on the artist's intent and context when the work was created. Thus it denies that a work of art needs or possesses a predetermined, intrinsic, immutable structure. It asserts that, in art, there are no rules and strictures, no right or wrong, only limitless interpretative possibility.

Importing this literary criticism theory into architecture, deconstructivist architects—some denied the decon label as yet another example of society's imposing rules—saw it as an intellectual justification for challenging or rejecting conventional principles of composition, both traditional and modern. Their aspiration was to invent a new, autonomous architecture liberated from the con-

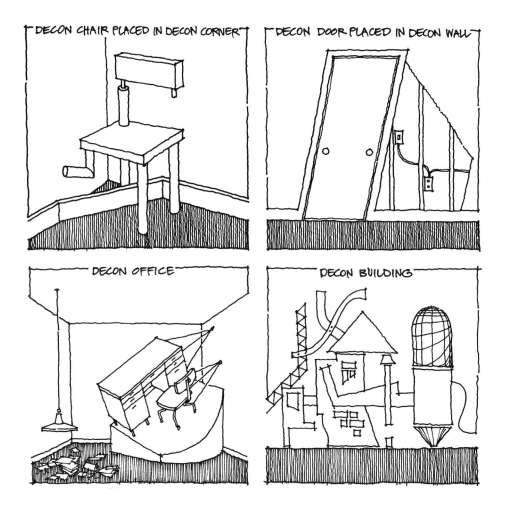

DECON CHAIR PLACED IN DECON CORNER

DECON DOOR PLACED IN DECON WALL

DECON OFFICE

DECON BUILDING

straints of aesthetic style and recognized design and construction practices. The modern condition, they argued, demands an exploration, acceptance, and celebration of the realities of society's chaos and imperfection. Let buildings express directly ideas of disorder and confusion, collision and conflict, ambiguity and uncertainty. Accordingly, decon architecture visually embodies all of these attributes. And decon architects freely pursue their highly personal design interests, impulses, and whims, much like an avant-garde painter or sculptor might, unfettered by tradition.

Of course, decon quickly became another kind of design style, although one difficult to characterize. Many decon buildings look as if they suddenly were frozen in the process of exploding or imploding, collapsing or shattering apart, melting down or dissolving. Walls, ceilings, columns, and beams are often not orthogonal to each other. Surfaces may be tilted, warped, or oddly shaped. Diverse volumes are arbitrarily juxtaposed. Many elements may seem purposeless, functionally or structurally gratuitous. Other elements seem to be colliding with each other, fusing together or blasting each other apart. Decon buildings are often collages of visual perverseness and instability and, at the same time, of extraordinary visual complexity and excitement. They are provocative and newsworthy simply because they are so different, so radical, so disdainful of the rules. Ironically, most could not have been designed or constructed without computers and sophisticated CAD software. For these reasons, decon philosophy can be very appealing to architecture students naturally tempted by decon's computer-generated, in-your-face forms.

Sociology and Psychology

At most American universities, introductory courses in sociology and psychology are available, and many architectural schools advise students to take them. After all, since architects must design environments mostly for people, it seems reasonable that they understand how and why people behave as they do. Moreover, during the past one hundred years, our exploration and knowledge of human behavior have increased substantially. Taking note of this, some architectural educators have tried to teach design based explicitly on the analysis and interpretation of human behavior. But except for a few years in the 1960s and 1970s, the study of human behavior has never been a mainstream research or pedagogical interest for design faculty or architecture students.

Nevertheless, because an essential purpose of architecture is to serve people, to accommodate human activity and respond to human needs, architects routinely consider how occupants and users of designed environments will feel and act. Design for special population groups, such as the elderly, the learning disabled, the hospitalized, or the imprisoned, requires extensive knowledge of user characteristics. As a result architects today can be more effective in designing facilities for these populations with extensive information, gained through both experience and structured research, about individual and group behavior of such users.

Senior citizens, for example, generally prefer to furnish their own apartments and surround themselves with their personal mementos, furniture, and belongings—as much as they can reasonably fit into the space available. Elderly residents like to sit and look outside, to watch activity in neighboring spaces or abutting streets. Further the elderly are sensitive to temperature, tolerating thermal variations, drafts, and humidity much less than younger residents. To the architect designing a dwelling for elderly users, such factors suggest an apartment with ample wall space for furniture and wall hangings, large windows for looking outside, and high-performance insulating glass to reduce heat loss, drafts, and thermal discomfort. Still, no amount of computer time, research, or user interviews can alter the fact that, as always, the architect must finally mediate between these potentially conflicting requirements, ultimately making subjective judgments for proportioning and positioning windows.

Sociological and psychological research also deals with perception and stimulus-response relationships that can inform architectural design decisions. For example, many architects rely on personal taste or follow fashion trends to select colors. But some, knowing that certain colors provoke specific kinds of reactions, select accordingly. The effects of noise, levels of illumination, and thermal comfort are well known and have influenced the design of work environments such as offices and factories. The need for privacy has influenced the design of the workplace, hospitals, and schools. Again, the architect must mediate between conflicting objectives, willfully devising an aesthetic strategy.

Functionalism

Many architects and teachers of architecture profess functionalism above all. They are viewed as being pragmatic, down to earth in their advocacy, eschewing fantasy and speculation. Their guiding philosophy is to make buildings that "work," that efficiently accommodate the uses intended, are structurally stable, environmentally comfortable, cost-effective, and, by virtue of being functional, also attractive.

Functionalism can include or complement morphology, technology, sociology, and psychology but does not begin consciously with the willful act of producing form for form's sake. Rather, functionalists generally claim that if the architect succeeds at making a building that works, then it will be beautiful and artful automatically, and inevitably, without overtly striving for artistic effect.

Functionalism places great emphasis on the client's program and other project constraints as the determinants of architectural form. Accordingly site and climatic conditions, circulation and space requirements, building codes, construction methods, and budget limitations are stressed as decision-making criteria, among others. Design proposals are evaluated pragmatically. Style is assumed to be derivative, that is, the result of a series of rational decisions about massing, spatial organization, structure, materials, fenestration, and proportioning. To many, functionalism is synonymous with modernism.

For the architectural student, functionalism may be one of the easiest philosophies to understand and apply in the studio. It appears to be analytical, logical, straightforward, an extension of the kinds of thinking and problem solving experienced earlier in primary and secondary school, and in life in general. It does not rely on highly abstract or intellectually arcane theories of design. It is transferable readily from project to project as a design strategy. It could be applied to the design of a toll booth as well as to a museum. It is always contemporary, since it does not preclude the architect's willful application of up-to-date stylistic embellishments, as long as they seem to fit.

The fallacy of pure functionalism is that it ignores the nonfunctional dimensions of architecture—psychic, emotional, intellectual, visual—that are difficult to quantify or specify in a program. They may be consciously provided by the designer, but sometimes they appear by accident or as an afterthought. Whatever their source, these architectural qualities are the ones that make buildings more than just buildings that work. Ironically, many inspired architects, although not perceived to be of the functionalist school, indeed practice functionalism, but always in combination with some other aesthetic philosophy.

Methodology

Somewhat related to functionalism is the professing of methodology as an end in itself. Focusing on how one produces rather than on what one produces, methodological architects and teachers are interested in process and its management per se. Methodology holds a certain fascination for them—more so than aesthetic exploration and invention. Methodologies can relate to design and graphic techniques, computers and software, administration, project management, finance, and business development.

Methodologists create diagrams, work schedules, charts, and data surveys. They study decision theory, computer modeling and simulation, cost accounting, value engineering, marketing, and personnel management, among others. By understanding and mastering the process by which work is produced, they argue, the quality of the product will be automatically enhanced. Moreover, efficiency and cost savings will be achieved. Improved methods equal improved products.

Allied with other compatible philosophies and willpower, methodology can help in coping with architecture's uncertainties and complexities. But like any of the -isms and -ologies already cited, excessive preoccupation with the how at the expense of the why can lead to compromised results. No matter how rational our approach to architecture, we still need wisdom and inspiration based on human values and personal convictions, which vary with time, place, culture, and circumstances.

Ecology

We are part of the natural environment, yet we often think of ourselves as battling nature. Often heard phrases describe our perceived

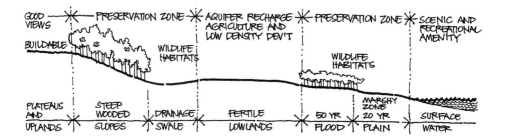

relationship to the natural environment: humankind against nature, against the sea, conquering nature, struggling against the elements or against nature . . . don't "fool with mother nature." Buildings are "shelters" whose purpose is to separate us from nature, allowing us to survive inclemency. Therefore it is not surprising that architects are concerned with how their designs relate to the natural setting, and some have taken nature itself as the generator of building form.

The ecology in which a building exists comprises a number of ecosystems. The atmosphere above the earth's surface contains gases, water vapor, and particles. The hydrosphere is the network of oceans, seas, lakes, and rivers, both above and below the earth's surface, made up of water. The lithosphere is the earth's crust—the soils, minerals, and rock formations at and below the surface. Pervading all of these is the biosphere—the animal and plant life native to each region of the earth. Climate—that combination of wind, precipitation, temperature, humidity, and atmospheric pressure—is the natural result of the interaction of the sun with the earth's ecosystems.

The elements of nature, however, do not tell how to design architecture until humans intervene. That intervention traditionally manifests itself somewhere between two extremes. At one extreme is the building thoroughly integrated with nature, married to the landscape and its specific site. This kind of building uses local materials and makes forms echoing the character of the site. Exemplifying this are hillside, cliffside, and underground dwellings found in Asia and Africa. They become almost indistinguishable from the earth and environment in which they sit. Some of the regional architecture of the American southwest illustrates this organic approach as well.

Architects inclined toward nature profess not only respect for ecology but also physical design that takes formal cues from the specific ecology at hand. Such designs are thus shaped by the landscape and the climate. Indigenous materials, native to the site, are used. The architecture must be in harmony with the site, unobtrusive and minimally destructive of the land and life-forms found there. Highest priority is given to saving trees, minimizing excavation or filling of land, avoiding interference with the natural flow of water, and employing the sun and wind directly to temper the constructed environment.

At the other extreme are buildings that stand in sharp contrast to the natural setting, in no way emulating or blending with the natural environment. Architecture and site coexist in an equilibrium of juxtaposition and complementarity, each asserting itself against the other without yielding unreasonably. There is no attempt to camouflage. Usually such buildings stand as dominant objects, marking the ground where civilization has tamed nature. The Taj Mahal, the Empire State Building, and Dulles Airport are such buildings.

Whether a building merges with or dominates its site, another ecological consideration impels some architects and educators: sustainability. Striving for sustainability implies design and construction with minimal consumption of natural resources and energy, consumption that can adversely affect the well-being of the earth's environment. Architecture demands huge investments of materials and energy, for both construction and operation. Extracting from the earth, processing, manufacturing, transporting, installing, finishing, and maintaining every item in a built project, from roads to roofing, has an environmental cost. Consequently, if architects could assess these environmental costs for a given design and then minimize them, they could contribute significantly to sustaining ecological health. For a few architects, sustainable design has become an ethical imperative.

Urbanism

In cities and suburbs, a multitude of other forces come into play that render a philosophy of environmentalism or sustainability, taken alone, inadequate to the task of design. Accordingly, urbanism encompasses a range of theories and principles applicable to the creation of urban settlement patterns and the civic spaces and buildings of which they are comprised. Subscribed to by many architects, some of whom specialize in planning and urban design, urbanism is predicated on the fundamental belief that cities and urban spaces are the ultimate achievement of good architecture. Good buildings are fine, but they must contribute to making good towns and cities.

What makes a good town or city? Most proponents of urbanism would say that good cities are vibrant centers of life: commerce and trade, habitation, cultural activity, education, recreation and entertainment, and production. A well-designed urban environment facilitates and encourages the interaction of people from all walks of life; provides networks for diverse modes of transportation; has a variety of building types—some civic and monumental, some quietly in the background; has identifiable neighborhoods; and has within it a hierarchy of streets, ranging from boulevards to alleys, plus public squares and parks. There would be a variety of dwelling types exhibiting a wide range of size, style, location, and cost. Urbanism advocates mixed-use development, combining residential, commercial, cultural, and recreational uses, rather than segregating these uses into separate zones or areas of cities.

Most architects who subscribe to urbanism use European cities and towns as their models, although they also extol the virtues of nineteenth-century American towns. Using examples such as Paris, Rome, Amsterdam, Savannah, or Charleston, they admire both the traditional streetscape patterns and the pedestrian-friendliness of these places. They point to their piazzas and spacious avenues; civic squares and public gardens; intimate, narrow streets and passageways; venerable old buildings (churches, town halls, palaces, museums, stately as well as modest dwellings), some serving as visual landmarks in the urban fabric; well-proportioned courtyards within buildings; intense sidewalk activity, including eating and drinking; rhythmic arcades or colonnades lining streets and plazas; and frequently a common palette of building materials, giving both unity and variety to what otherwise might be a visually chaotic collection of individual structures. They like places where pedestrians compete successfully with automobiles, and there is a mixture of shops, apartments, and public outdoor spaces.

Urbanism condemns much of suburbia and metropolitan sprawl, citing among their ills visual formlessness, automobile dependency and absence of public transit, single-use zoning, social isolation and alienation, and lack of a sense of place or community. The characteristics of sprawl include congested, unattractive commercial

strip highways, excessively wide subdivision streets, and unfathomable, circuitous road networks. Contemporary urbanism also condemns previous urban design principles that have been widely discredited, although not discarded. Much American zoning law still embodies some of the modernist, utopian ideas about cities that held sway between the 1920s and 1960s. During that period, prevailing urban theories advocated what has come to pass in so many newer American cities: strict separation of land uses into zones and enclaves interconnected by high-speed freeways, with low-density land uses spread across vast metropolitan regions.

Urbanism in recent decades, like the historic preservation movement, has sensitized many architects, directly influencing how they design urban buildings. Prior to the 1970s, architects often designed a building as an autonomous object to be shaped or sculpted at will by the architect, sometimes ignoring the urban context of the site. Building form was constrained only by its budget and functional program, zoning regulations, available technology, and the client's demands. Relating visually to the size, scale, geometry, materials, and details of surrounding buildings was often a secondary consideration. But architects began to appreciate the importance of context. They discovered that context could help shape a building, and, at the same time, a building could harmonize with and positively enhance its context. Of course, contextualism can be overdone, as sometimes happens when an architect literally replicates neighboring buildings, which may not be worthy of replication, just to fit in.

Clearly urbanism is fueled in part by romanticism and nostalgia for an idealized past, and some who profess urbanism also profess historicism. But most architects and urbanists agree that modern cities and suburbs have been badly crafted, with something of value lost since the middle of the twentieth century. Without rejecting technology or the private car or economic realities, urbanism seeks to discover and apply principles of urban design that can help restore civic vitality to American cities and neighborhoods.

Symbology

One of the most controversial but persistent philosophies of design teaches that architecture is a medium, like poetry or painting, for the transmission of messages. Architecture can communicate ideas or information that the designer-author wishes to express and convey through building. According to some, this may be the highest plateau of achievement and meaning in architecture: the plateau of symbology. Architecture must stand for something. It is not sufficient only to provide shelter, facilitate work, produce a return on investment, or look good. Architecture must transmit something meaningful to the senses and minds of those who interact with it, who "read" it.

There is no limit to the kinds of things that can be symbolized. For example, buildings can be designed to be mystical, to represent spiritual or theological concepts, of which Gothic cathedrals are a splendid example. Architecture can be rhetorical, preaching specific beliefs or causes through particular use of styles, ornamentation, and forms. For example, Roman classicism was embraced by both fascists and communists in Europe in the 1930s as the style of architecture best suited to express to people the fundamental dignity, nobility, and correctness of each respective political philosophy. The very same style in capitalistic America was seen to be especially appropriate for banks.

Metaphoric architecture abounds. Buildings can represent or stand for other buildings in other places. In the early years of the American republic, the Parthenon, symbol of Greek democracy, was a source of architectural inspiration. Buildings can symbolize nature, or people and their activities, struggles and victories. The Washington Monument and Eiffel Tower are well-known symbolic structures. The former, modeled after an Egyptian obelisk (obelisks have been fashionable for centuries), memorializes a man but symbolizes a nation. The latter, while demonstrating the achievements of engineering, has become the universally recognized symbol of Paris. Eero Saarinen's air terminal buildings at Kennedy and Dulles airports symbolize flight by appearing to be in flight.

Buildings can generate responses in observers through symbolic association. They can make us feel secure by being like nests or wombs—intimate, cozy, human scaled, soft to the touch. They can make us feel humble by being like giants: huge, heavy, hard, overpowering. Buildings can be endowed with wit and humor, as evident in many architectural follies, or they can be apocalyptic, like many deconstructivist edifices. The most common form of message delivery through symbolism is the use of historical allusions and references in buildings. Such architecture may say: "I am unquestionably a new, twentieth-century building, but since modern architecture is so sterile, I am going to offer you transformed architectural motifs and elements from the past to which you can better relate: an Ionic column here, egg and dart molding there, multipaned double-hung windows." Like historicism, this approach reveres traditions from the past but uses them symbolically rather than literally, avoiding authentic reproduction.

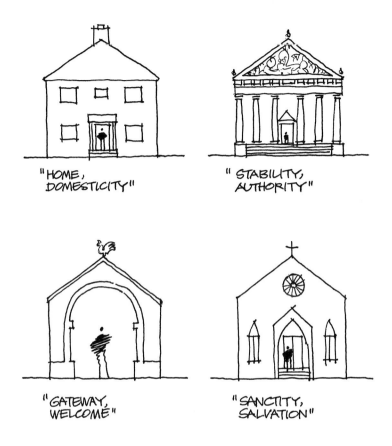

"HOME, DOMESTICITY"

"STABILITY, AUTHORITY"

"GATEWAY, WELCOME"

"SANCTITY, SALVATION"

In its own way, much of the architecture produced by the modern movement in the twentieth century was symbolic, even though many have thought it to be devoid of meaning or symbolism. After World War I, architects in Europe, and later in the United States, believed that a new architecture was needed to express the spirit and values of what they perceived to be a new age. This new age was heralded by the arrival of new social and political orders (primarily socialism and democracy), new technologies and machines, and new economics. For these architects, this meant new building functions and building types never before encountered and building on a much greater, mass-production scale. It seemed only logical to symbolize the aspirations of the new age through architectural expression.

To achieve this, modern architecture abandoned traditional motifs to look for a new symbolic language. The new age implied efficiency, standardization, and repetition. It was to be a machine age but also an age of unprecedented individual freedom. Some buildings began to look efficient: less ornate, plainer in detail, simpler in form. Some became more systematized in their appearance. Still others, exploiting new materials and construction methods, became exuberant and complex in form, symbolizing the freedom of expression presumably encouraged in the new age. Historical styles no longer seemed relevant. The new symbology was predicated on theories of functionalism and technology: buildings should look like what they are or do, expressing on the outside the function of the inside and their mode of construction.

Modernism, though no longer a rebellious movement, is still with us. Some architects continue to profess its rightness and appropriateness as the only legitimate, symbolic way to go. They argue for symbolic universality, for buildings expressing their function in ways that can be read by anybody anywhere. They design churches that say "church," houses that say "home," office buildings that say "office building," or factories that say "factory." They reject the contemporary use of an Ionic column because, to them, it cartoons a past form whose shape arose from technical, social, cultural, and aesthetic conditions no longer in existence.

You, the reader, must now ponder these abbreviated observations about architectural professors and what they profess. If still moved by the prospects of becoming an architect, the next chapter will help you select professors through the choice of a school.

6

Architectural Schools:
Choosing and Being Chosen

It is one thing to present general descriptions of architectural programs and professors and quite another to suggest how to go about choosing a specific school. Further, what should one do to prepare for architectural school, and for getting admitted?

Preparing for Architectural School

No matter what kind of program in architecture seems appealing, most schools demand similar kinds of academic experience, knowledge, and abilities: aptitude in drawing and graphics; creative talent evidenced by work in art or design; aptitude in basic mathematics (algebra, trigonometry, geometry, introductory calculus) and science, particularly physics; basic computer skills; verbal aptitude as evidenced through reading, writing, and oral expression; and some cultural interests and awareness.

Whether through coursework or extracurricular initiative, any experience creating two- or three-dimensional art is beneficial to the prospective architect. Contrary to popular assumptions, *mechanical drawing or drafting of high school or vocational school variety is not the most valuable kind of graphic experience prior to studying architecture.* Indeed, these can be hindrances if they lead to "mechanical" thinking. This results from the emphasis in such courses on techniques of drafting rather than on design principles and creative composition.

The development of freehand drawing and sketch techniques is far more valuable at the outset of architectural school. Courses or exercises that focus on spatial perception and representation are recommended over drafting or mechanical drawing. Work in traditional art—painting, drawing, sculpture—will contribute to the mastery of architectural design and drawing skills. Experience in the visual arts, whether representational or abstract, creative or applied, develops visual thinking essential to being an architect.

Visual thinking and sensitivity may also be developed through seeing and reading about architecture. Those who have taken the time to travel and look at buildings and cities, and to think about them, will be a step ahead. You do not necessarily have to travel far, since you interact with architecture every day, no matter where you are. There are many introductory books about architecture, and design is periodically a topic of articles in newspapers and magazines.

Because architecture is so integral to the history of civilization and is so directly concerned with human activities and needs, studies in the humanities are valuable preparation for architectural education. History and philosophy of Western civilization are particularly relevant. Courses in literature, English composition, and foreign languages hone skills of analysis and expression, of great value to the architect. Even the study of music is appropriate; recall that Renaissance architects believed music to be a "mathematical art" whose rules of harmony and consonance formed the basis for architectural composition.

In addition to the humanities, introductory courses or readings in the social sciences—economics, sociology, psychology, or anthropology—are pertinent to the education of an architect. Excursions through the fields of humanities and social sciences can continue during architectural school, but time will be limited, so it is wise to pursue them before embarking on three or four years of intense architectural concentration.

Before jumping into architectural school, try to visit an architect's office and talk with architects in practice. Here you will get a sense of the physical environment in which architects work, what they do from hour to hour, and the kinds of projects they produce. Many will freely offer advice about the profession, schools, other firms, and even other careers.

Choosing Schools

This is a big decision. Many factors must be considered in choosing which architectural schools to apply to and then, if admitted, which one to attend. Following are the most pertinent criteria, although not necessarily in order of importance.

Location

Where is it? City, suburb, town, or country? A school's location is vital to its health, for it partly determines the school's ambience and relationship to the larger world. Schools in cities have access to cultural activities and become urban cultural resources themselves. City schools have urban design laboratories at their doorsteps. They can become intimately involved in the urban design issues of the city they belong to, even influencing policy and helping solve real city problems. They can readily draw on the resources of the city, inviting people from the city into the school to

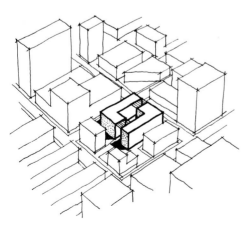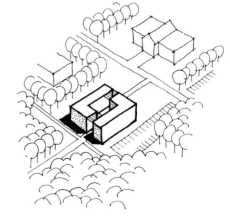

A very urban school; a very suburban school.

teach, lecture, or evaluate work. The University of California at Berkeley, the University of Utah in Salt Lake City, Rice University in Houston, Washington University in St. Louis, Harvard and MIT in Cambridge, Yale in New Haven, the University of Pennsylvania in Philadelphia, and Columbia University in New York City are city-based schools with strong urban ties.

Other schools reside in more idyllic settings, on campuses located away from cities, often in college towns—for example. Princeton, the University of Virginia in Charlottesville, Cornell in Ithaca, and the University of Michigan in Ann Arbor. Students at such schools face fewer off-campus distractions, although being located away from major cities does not mean deprivation. Students in suburban or exurban schools consider urban design problems with equal vigor, but they have farther to go to tap urban resources. The greatest difference between schools located in or out of cities has to do with the quality of extracurricular life. In New York, San Francisco, and Chicago there are more movies, theaters, restaurants, museums, clubs, shops, bookstores, libraries, schools—the amenities of urban life—than elsewhere.

Program Type

Which type of program is suitable? Are you going to study architecture at the undergraduate or graduate level? If you are entering college as a freshman knowing that architecture is to be your major, you will have to make a choice. Do you want to pursue a five-year, professional B.Arch. degree, the most direct and economical route to a professional degree, but also the most intense with the fewest options? Would it be more prudent to pursue a four-year B.S. or B.A. degree, majoring in architecture, and then go for two or three more years of graduate school to earn the M.Arch degree? This takes longer and is more expensive, but it also offers much greater flexibility—to take more electives, explore other fields, mature, change majors without losing time, and take time off to work between undergraduate and graduate studies.

Answering these questions may depend on your educational background and other factors not related directly to program type.

However, keep in mind a practical consideration: more and more graduate architects are receiving masters degrees as their *first* professional degree. This may be an advantage in initially finding jobs and getting higher pay, especially in government employment, over peers holding B.Arch. degrees.

If you are beginning your architectural studies as a graduate student, consider carefully the organization and duration of the M.Arch. curriculum. How many calendar years will it take? (Be sure to count semesters. Programs offering a three-year master's degree may require at least two summers of studio work, since fully accredited programs often take seven to eight semesters to complete.) Be wary of schools promising graduate students with no previous architecture school experience a master's degree in fewer than three years. If a thesis is required, most graduate programs take closer to four years to complete.

Reputation

Let us not pretend that a school's reputation is unimportant. Schools have reputations, deserved or undeserved, and such reputations influence who attends and, to some extent, what becomes of them as graduates. Of course there are different kinds of reputations to be had, but most are academic in nature. People think of universities such as Harvard, Yale, Princeton, Cal Tech, Columbia, Cornell, and MIT as academically first rate, with top students and faculty, high admission and grading standards, fat endowments, and distinguished alumni. But many universities have departments or programs whose individual reputations may exceed the reputation of the university as a whole or, conversely, not live up to the university's reputation. This is often the case in public universities where specific disciplines have been well supported. Other reputations are related to quality-of-life characteristics— small, big, personal, impersonal, socially oriented (parties, fraternities), or pastoral—which are usually independent of their strictly academic reputations within respective fields. For example, a university may have a reputation as a party school yet also have many outstanding academic departments.

The potential fallacy in choosing a school based on reputation is that its reputation may not be deserved. Architectural schools experience turnover in faculty, frequently tinker with their courses and curricula, and periodically modify their goals and directions. The arrival or departure of one or two key professors can make a big difference for a school whose reputation has been built primarily on a specific teacher's fame and ability to attract students. Or a dean and faculty may adopt a new educational direction, inappropriate or irrelevant for many students. For these reasons, there is a long history of architectural programs at very good universities fluctuating in quality, even from year to year. Therefore prospective students must be certain that both the university *and* the architectural school within it have reputations that reflect current conditions, to the extent that reputation is a factor in selection.

Increasing numbers of architecture schools at state universities have developed top-quality programs taught by first-rate faculty, with excellent resources and physical facilities. Often overlooked or underrated by superficial attempts to compare schools (such as the rankings compiled annually by *U.S. News and World Report*—see the commentary in the Afterword), these programs not only are financial bargains, they also produce graduates who are excelling and leading the profession. Long gone are the days when you had to be an alumnus of an Ivy League school to succeed in the architectural profession.

No matter what school you choose, you ultimately will be a graduate of that institution, a lifetime member of a network of alumni. This reflects the real difference between most universities: the students. If you are a student at Yale, you will be surrounded by a much higher percentage of gifted students than if you are a student at a state university. Thus even a Yale graduate who was academic mediocrity personified may still survive and succeed because he or she belongs to the Yale network and because there are people to whom origins and networks matter. Nevertheless, for substance, you must dig deeper than networks and reputation. You must get first-hand, up-to-date information.

Resources

Does the school have that combination of tangibles—money for faculty and operations, classroom and studio space, libraries, computers, and other equipment—necessary to run an acceptable program in architecture? This is one of the questions posed when architectural schools are accredited, and students should ask it too. The only way to ascertain this is to visit the school, read its catalog carefully, and talk to its dean, chair, admissions director, faculty, and students. What is the student-teacher ratio, particularly in the studio courses? Each design studio teacher should have no more than fifteen to eighteen students; twelve to fourteen is desirable; fewer than twelve would be a luxury and more than eighteen would be excessive, unless there are graduate teaching assistants.

Is there sufficient staff—secretaries, librarians, curators, graduate assistants—to support the program and keep the place operating smoothly day to day? Lack of staff can seriously impair the effectiveness and administration of a program in architecture. Look at the architecture library. Does it seem ample in size and readily accessible? What about the computer lab? Ask the students. Check out the slide collection and the availability of audiovisual equipment. These are essential to any architectural program of quality.

Look at the physical environment where you will be spending tremendous amounts of time. Is there sufficient space for design tables, model making, exhibition, and group reviews? In addition to studios, there should be spaces dedicated to conducting seminars and small- to medium-sized lecture courses, and an auditorium for lectures and film or slide presentations. Is there some kind of public exhibition gallery associated with the school? Are there conference rooms and adequate offices for the faculty and staff? Even the quality of lighting and the acoustic environment are worth noting.

Is there a shop equipped for making models or furniture, in either wood or metal? How about a materials testing lab for experimenting with structural elements or models? A photographic darkroom and photo studio and facilities for reproducing drawings (ozalid printing)? And plenty of storage for the work of students?

Only a visit to the school will yield the answers to questions concerning resources and reputation. Facilities vary in quality from school to school, but all of them should exist or be accessible in some form. Many architectural schools have their own, separate buildings on campus, while others are embedded more impersonally in university megabuildings or building fragments left over from earlier times. The latter are sometimes the softest kind of environment to work in; aging buildings do not imply program senility.

Cost

The cost of education has reached such levels that almost no one can disregard it as a school selection factor. There is a point of diminishing returns in expending tuition fees for quality in education. In other words, spending twice as much does not increase educational or career payback twofold. Therefore every student and family must carefully weigh the benefits of educational expense against other alternatives, including pursuing educational alternatives outside the traditional university.

There is little choice today about attending architectural school if you want to be an architect, but there is a choice as to cost. The primary choice is between public and private education. The American system of publicly supported state universities has grown in both size and quality during the past several decades. Because state universities enjoy the support and relative stability of continuing, legislated budgets, they have been able to weather the cyclical pressures of economic recession and inflation. In turn they have not experienced threatening drops in enrollments and tuition revenue on which most private universities depend. Further, they have not had to increase their tuition fees at the same rate as private institutions.

Therefore students should carefully compare the tuition and living costs of those schools they are considering. They must also take into account the availability of student financial aid and loans. Many universities offer substantial scholarships, fellowships, and teaching or research assistantships (for graduate students) that can significantly mitigate the tuition costs. But each university differs in its student aid strategy, and these should be closely scrutinized, along with the competition.

Students

Who goes to the school you are considering? What kind of students are they, and what kind of architects do they become? Never underestimate the impact on program quality attributable to student quality. Good students are attracted to what they perceive as good schools and programs; they want to be with esteemed mentors and peers. This is a distinct advantage enjoyed by schools with strong reputations, since reputation alone automatically attracts outstanding students and faculty.

It is also true that there are outstanding students in every program, students who would excel wherever they might enroll. It then becomes a matter of percentages and ambience. At state universities, a large percentage of the student body will be of decidedly average ability. To a large extent, these students will establish the academic ambience and generally perceived student intellectual level within the institution and its classrooms.

By contrast, most of those students of average ability would not be admitted at selective private universities. This does not mean that the programs and faculty at state universities are inferior. In fact, they may be superior, lacking only in reputation. The outstanding student at a state university may stand out even more. But he or she will find the overall student intellectual climate less stimulating, on the whole, than it would be at a highly reputed university. Most architectural schools control admission to and retention within their own programs, applying standards of performance frequently more stringent than those of other disciplines. Thus even at many big state universities filled with students just passing through, the intellectual climate in the architectural school can be quite heady.

Faculty

An architectural school is no better than its faculty, but you cannot judge the quality of a school's faculty just by reading the catalog or listing their collective degrees or universities attended. You must inquire. There are many sources: students already in the program, graduates of the program, practicing architects who know the faculty and program, other teachers in other departments or schools, and the faculty themselves, most of whom are quite willing to tell you how good they are.

But what do you want to know? What do the faculty teach, and how do they teach it? Are they dedicated to their work? Do they show concern for their students, for what they are learning? What do they do outside the classroom or studio: practice, conduct research, write, travel, lecture? Have they gained local, regional, or national recognition or reputations individually? Are people stimulated listening to them? Do they demand the best of their students, and do they invest time and energy preparing to teach? Are they in touch with the real as well as the academic world? Above all, are they continuing to grow and learn themselves, to innovate and question, while professing fully and competently the subject matter for which they are responsible?

A number of architectural school faculties have individual members who are considered names or stars. They are usually architects, architectural historians, or theoreticians with national or international reputations for their work or ideas. Teaching is often only one of several activities in which these faculty members engage. Their status as academic or professional celebrities is believed to bring comparable status to the institutions where they teach. Indeed, their presence does draw students, since students can easily imagine and anticipate that some of the master's aura and insights will be transferable. For example, Colin Rowe, well known as a teacher and theoretician in architectural circles, attracted graduate students for years to Cornell. Louis Kahn's studio at the University of Pennsylvania attracted and produced hundreds of disciples during the 1950s and 1960s. It was not the topics of their courses that drew the students but rather their personal design philosophies and approach to teaching. Regardless of other program characteristics, the presence of a known and respected faculty member can be a great asset to a school and its students.

Nevertheless, there can be a danger in chasing stars. Frequently their time and commitment to teaching and interacting with students are limited. Extrauniversity obligations may keep them away from the classroom or studio or may compete for their attention even when they are there. They may teach only a small number of students in advanced courses, perhaps only one semester per year, so that relatively few students in a school's population ever participate in featured courses. And occasionally these superstars are less than super as teachers. They may have grown stale, bored, and boring, they may be espousing philosophies or ideas that no longer seem relevant or applicable. In any event look closely at who is getting top billing, and get reviews from currently enrolled students and recent graduates.

Prospective architectural students having specific interests related to architecture should seek schools with faculty members who share and pursue those interests. Try to discover who is focused on the issues that interest you (such as historic preservation, housing, landscape design, interiors, construction, computer-aided design, or history, to name a few of the possible areas of specialization and research). There could be no one sharing your interests, which you would want to know before making a decision.

These questions will never be fully answered until you are actually in school, but you will get some sense of a faculty's quality by probing a bit. Unfortunately most students rarely know what their faculty is all about before enrolling in an architectural school, and a few do not know even when they finish.

Program Directions

Yet another key characteristic differentiates one school of architecture from another: the school's direction, or the dominant academic ethos that can infuse an institution. An architecture dean and like-minded faculty collectively can and often do emphasize certain philosophies and theories of design, certain kinds of problems and projects, and even certain ways of thinking and looking at the world. Even while satisfying requirements all schools must meet to maintain professional degree accreditation, a school of architecture can have its own spin—its own discernable tone and orientation.

At Syracuse University, for example, the architecture school was led for years by Dean Werner Seligman, an architect who stamped his imprint almost indelibly on a generation of Syracuse students and faculty. Seligman's personal, strongly modernist design attitudes, language, and graphic approach permeated the school, in keeping with the master-apprentice tradition. Diversity in design thinking was minimal. Faculty taught and students designed à la Seligman, and studio projects naturally reflected Seligman's powerful tutelage. Similar circumstances prevailed for decades after World War II at the Illinois Institute of Technology in Chicago, where Ludwig Mies van der Rohe was the resident guru. Students came to IIT to learn how to design like Mies, despite the presence of other faculty, and anyone uninterested in Miesian design would have found it pointless to be at IIT.

Other schools focus differently. MIT's architecture program always has traveled in diverse topical directions, but with periodic shifts. At various times it has emphasized urban design, energy conservation, construction technology, housing and community design, and design methodology. At this writing, computer-aided design and design visualization are occupying center stage. By contrast, Princeton's school of architecture focuses primarily on issues of form and form making, on intellectual speculation and verbalization seemingly as important as visualization. Despite its theoretical direction, Princeton's design faculty often are celebrated practitioners.

Notre Dame's architecture school revived classicism and pedagogical traditions of the Ecole des Beaux Arts. At Howard University, many of whose students are African American or come from abroad, design studios often undertake projects in economically deprived communities or in foreign countries. Other schools push technology-inspired, constructivist and deconstructivist design, treating architecture more like art with little explicit concern for social, environmental, or economic development issues. Still others, such as Harvard and the University of Maryland, are strongly directed toward urban design, landscape architecture, and the study of architectural and urban history. There remain a few schools, still allied with engineering colleges, offering a decided engineering and construction research bias, but their numbers have diminished.

Find out, before selecting a school, in what directions a school is headed, being mindful that a school can change directions in just a few years. Query students, faculty, and architects to get a clear and current picture. Knowing about program direction is crucial, since your school's direction probably will be the direction you follow once you begin your academic journey into architecture.

The Admissions Process

You've looked at architectural schools, asked lots of questions, and decided where you would like to study. How do you get admitted? What is the application process like? Each architectural school has its own system for processing applicants and will provide appropriate application forms and guidelines. Nevertheless, there are several things to do and keep in mind when applying to architectural school, independent of particular school requirements. These involve little extra efforts demonstrating clearly your strengths and the merits of your application.

The Portfolio

Many schools require submission of a portfolio showing examples of the applicant's creative work. Portfolios typically contain photographs, drawings, and prints or slides depicting the applicant's efforts in art, design, or drafting. Sometimes it is the portfolio itself—how it is prepared and assembled, its look and graphic quality—that gets the admission committee's attention. Seldom can an admissions committee predict future performance from an applicant's portfolio content, but if the portfolio is well presented and conveys the sense that the author might really think like an architect or designer, it can make a positive impression on the committee—even more than the design achievements illustrated within. Of course, the better the design work, the more positive the impression.

Interviews

Many schools do not require a personal interview for admission. Disregard this nonrequirement. Go there anyway, not only to learn about the place but also to meet at least one or two faculty concerned with admissions. You are, after all, building a case for yourself. Without being pushy, try to convey to your interviewer your interest, motivation, background, and qualifications, and do so with sincerity and enthusiasm. Be engaging. Establish a dialogue in which you learn about the program, the faculty, and the interviewer (remember that architects like to talk about themselves) while the interviewer is learning about you. A few positive notes jotted down by that interviewer and placed in your application file can have great impact on an admission decision.

Reference Letters

Virtually all schools ask that you request teachers or others who know you and your work to send letters attesting to your character, skills, and academic qualifications. These letters can be very decisive but of little impact if they come from personal friends or relatives whose credentials or objectivity are doubtful. To make reference letters count, ask the writers to focus on your educational and professional achievements, your work habits, and your potential. The best letters are from employers or teachers who knew you well as a student. Citation of specific accomplishments, abilities, and outstanding personal characteristics will be most helpful to admissions committees. Finally, it is always a good idea for the writer to explain briefly his or her relationship to you: where, when, and in what circumstances.

Grades

There is no way around it: grades are very important. Apply with the highest grade point average you can muster. However, grades are not everything, and softness in course grades can sometimes be overcome by strengths elsewhere, especially portfolios, letters of reference, and exam scores or experience. It is not unusual for architectural schools to admit students with less than stellar academic records, but who show great potential through a combination of experience and creative talent exhibited in their portfolios. This is particularly true of applicants who have been out of school for a while.

Exams

These are required by most universities for admission, the Scholastic Aptitude Test (SAT) for undergraduate programs and the Graduate Record Exam (GRE) for graduate programs. Neither exam measures aptitude or skill directly related to architecture, but they do show general academic talent and give indications of how students can be expected to perform. Some preparation for these exams is possible, including guidance in the art of exam taking. If you feel uncertain about your examination prospects, consider programs and courses that target exam performance.

Timing

Since university schedules usually call for classes (and the academic year) to begin in the fall, the admissions process must commence almost a year earlier. Application deadlines occur in spring between January and March or April, and students are usually notified between March and May. Therefore applicants should visit schools initially in the fall, then prepare their portfolios and application forms prior to the submission deadline. Examination dates should be verified, and exams taken prior to the spring admissions review. Only in special circumstances do schools accept late applications. If you go for an interview, make sure it is before the admissions committee meets to consider applicants.

Financial Aid

When you apply, indicate your interest in financial aid directly on your application and in a cover letter as well. Many universities utilize standardized financial assistance applications processed separately from admissions applications. For graduate students, the budget process at many schools allocates fellowships, teaching assistantships, and work-study positions in late spring and summer. Therefore, let the school know of your interest in being considered for any or all of these. Also check into the availability of university scholarships or fellowships, which may not be administered by the school of architecture.

Admissions Odds

To how many schools should you apply? Presumably the more you try for, the higher the probability of being admitted by at least one. However, this strategy has practical limits of cost and time. I suggest the "rifle" rather than the "shotgun" approach. Apply only to those schools—perhaps three or four in number—in which you are genuinely interested, and add one more as a backup choice. Your backup should also be a school acceptable to you but for which admission is somewhat less competitive.

If you find yourself on a waiting list, be optimistic, since schools admit more students than they can actually enroll but then may fall short in enrollment a few weeks later, having expected more to accept admission. This is when they turn to their waiting list. If you are on a waiting list, there is no harm in writing the school about continued interest in attending. Help them keep you in mind.

If you cannot attend the school of your choice, you can begin studying architecture at your backup school, complete one or two years in good standing, and then transfer. This entails certain risks. First, without a strong record to support your transfer application, you still may not gain admission. Second, if admitted as a transfer, you may lose some course credits, or even a semester or two, in making the transfer between schools whose programs are not equivalent in content and quality. Third, to your pleasant surprise perhaps, you may prefer to finish your architectural studies where you started, having lost your desire to transfer to the school you originally preferred. This happens often because students settle into a program, become comfortable with familiar territory, and conclude that the backup school was better than they had expected.

Once admitted, reply to the school as soon as you have made your decision. There is usually an admission acceptance deadline, since it is critical to the school's planning to know how many intend to enroll in the coming year. If you need an extension while awaiting notice from other schools in which you are interested, write to request the extension. This is also the time to pose any still unanswered questions about financial aid, assistantships, transfer, or advance standing credits. Do not be surprised if some of these issues cannot be resolved until you arrive in the fall.

Feeling positive about yourself because somebody wants you, recall that the tough phase of architectural education is only just beginning. The next several years will be exciting, frustrating, mind expanding, enigmatic, amusing, tedious, exhausting, exhilarating, and outrageous all at the same time. Choosing and being chosen is only one of many milestones on the road to being an architect.

7

After School, What?

The successful completion of architectural school is a significant accomplishment and milestone in the career of any architect. The many years of intense study and demanding work at times seem to be unending. Only half of those who started may graduate. And yet although graduation signals the end of formal schooling, it is by no means a signal that your architectural education is complete.

In fact, as challenging as architectural school is, what follows may be far more challenging—not only because of continuing work load, competition, and complexity but also because graduate architects face a new array of choices and challenges that were not well understood before graduation. And every subsequent career path is a continuation of the architect's education, even if it does not entail traditional architectural practice. Therefore it is essential to look ahead and become aware of the options, remembering that education now simply shifts from the schoolroom to the workplace.

Internship

The majority of graduate architects, whether possessing a B.Arch. or M.Arch. degree, go from architectural school to architectural office. In many cases young architects have already acquired office experience working during summer vacations and part time during the academic year. These first few years of work in architects' offices are the internship years. The term is appropriate, for it clearly implies that the recently graduated architect is still being trained, still learning, still a student.

Architectural interns, like new arrivals in most professions, are usually overworked and paid comparatively little. They are overworked because they are energetic, eager to produce, hungry for new knowledge, and inexpensive to hire relative to more experienced architects. They are poorly paid because they are many in number competing for scarce positions, inexperienced technically, and frequently inefficient at performing unfamiliar tasks. Because the architectural fees that firms receive are often less than they should be, many firms cannot afford to pay very high salaries to anyone, especially novices.

The internship can be compared in limited ways to the internship physicians serve during their first year after medical school: lots of work and long hours for little pay. It can be justified as a way of getting paid for still being a student. In the United States, virtually every state requires that architects serve a specified period of internship before being eligible for licensing as an architect. The architectural profession has never been able to institutionalize its internship program like that of the medical profession, which has developed a national, competitive, computer-based system for evaluating and placing medical school graduates. Architectural interns still must make their own way, searching for and taking a job wherever they can find it. Consequently, completing architectural internship is solely in the hands of the intern.

Architectural employment is highly dependent on the economy, with the demand for new graduates fluctuating not only from year to year but also from month to month. A continuing, systematized internship program would require steady sources of employment, a unified process of intern-firm selection, match-up, assignment, and rigorous methods of evaluation. Economic uncertainties, coupled with the propensity of architects for resisting consensus on practically anything, particularly concerning their pocketbooks and their freedom of action, make the internship nothing more than the relationship established between individual interns and individual firms.

Internship requirements and standards nevertheless have been systematized, thanks to the efforts of the National Council of Architectural Registration Boards (NCARB). It has developed the Intern-Architect Development Program (IDP), which most state registration boards have adopted for licensing qualification. The IDP entails creating and maintaining a permanent file for each intern, but the intern is responsible for documenting his or her accumulated experience with each employer while maintaining contact with an IDP adviser who must be a licensed architect. Interns must accumulate stipulated, minimum amounts of time and experience performing different tasks. Considered integral to architectural practice, these diverse tasks are specifically defined and categorized by the IDP. Each of the intern's employers must certify that the intern satisfactorily performed the work in each category for the amount of time indicated and earned the points claimed. Thus the IDP goal is to ensure that every intern masters the full array of skills required for licensing and professional practice.

The equivalent of three full years of diversified internship experience, plus an accredited professional degree, are required by most states before examination and licensing. Fortunately, accumulated internship time does not have to be with one firm or within one state. Thus a new graduate architect must first compete for a job in the marketplace and then hope that jobs he or she gets will provide the mix of experience and training needed. Many graduate architects change jobs frequently during those initial years, whereas others stick with a single firm, perhaps hoping to become a senior employee or partner. Some work for small, edge-of-survival firms and others for large, established ones.

Graduate architects can acquire a great variety of skills and knowledge during internship, depending on the number of jobs held, type and size of firms worked for, type and size of projects designed, and responsibilities assumed. Some architectural interns are exposed immediately to a wide range of practical experience, including management experience. This is most common when employed during the internship years by relatively small firms (no more than five to ten professionals). On the other hand, most small firms do not have the opportunity to design projects large in scale and complexity.

Graduate architects who work for large firms may gain substantial experience focusing on specialized aspects of large projects but may not have the opportunity to gain the breadth of experience possible in the small office. Concentration and specialization often characterize the role of the intern architect in large practices, whereas diversification and generalization characterize many small practices. Additionally, large projects take longer to design and build than small projects, so over a three-year period, one might work on only two or three projects in a large firm but six or eight in a small firm. The intern in the large firm might never grasp the totality of a project and the integrative design process that are more apparent and accessible to the apprentice in the small firm. On the other hand, the young architect in the small office may not acquire the depth of experience achievable in bigger offices or have access to the range of expertise, methodologies, and resources found in many large, well-established firms.

One other critical variable related to firms is the willingness of senior architects—associates or principals—to spend time and energy teaching the intern architects they employ. Active and conscious teaching encompasses adequate discussion and explanation of design and technical issues, demonstration, exposure to clients and consultants, and, above all, delegation of responsibility without supervisory neglect. For the newly hired intern, senior architects are the surrogate mentors and professors left behind in architectural school. Therefore architectural offices sensitive to intern needs ensure that young architects, still eager to learn, acquire the knowledge and master the diverse skills necessary not only to satisfy internship requirements and pass the licensing examination, but also to practice architecture successfully.

Some licensing candidates approach the examination never having designed and built in steel or concrete or wood. Some have had little on-site construction experience or have never written specifications. Others may have found their internship years devoid of any substantial client contact or project management and contract administration responsibilities. Unfortunately, this reflects a reality of day-to-day practice in many firms that use personnel to the firm's best economic advantage. If someone is very good at doing CAD work, making models, designing construction details, or negotiating with contractors, there is a great temptation for the firm to continue assigning such tasks to that person regularly. Having mastered drafting or modeling software, an intern can find herself chained to a computer month after month without ever having the opportunity to perform the many other tasks architects must accomplish. This is the downside of specialization in architecture.

Given all of this, graduate architects should choose employment very thoughtfully, even if jobs are in short supply. The years of internship are extraordinarily formative. They not only prepare you (or fail to) for licensing and independent practice, but they also establish directions and attitudes that may shape much of your future career as an architect. Begin your career with a mediocre architect, and you will probably acquire mediocre habits of thought and production, no matter what your aspirations. Work in an office where good design is paramount and you are among talented designers, and you are likely to be inspired and to develop your own talents more fully. In fact, many outstanding firms have been founded by architects who worked for a number of years in a firm of the previous generation, a firm that wisely nurtured their strengths and abilities.

The ideal internship experience would consist of working for a small- to medium-sized firm doing high-quality design work, being assigned a multiplicity of tasks from conceptual sketching to contract documents to inspecting construction, and receiving a regular and adequate, if not generous, paycheck.

Becoming a Registered Architect

The process of becoming registered as an architect is another mini-ordeal on the way to becoming a full-fledged practitioner, and like graduation from architectural school, it too is a milestone. Once registered, you personally can offer architectural services to clients or become a principal of a firm. To become registered as an architect in the United States and to use the title "architect" legally, the common track is as follows:

1. Obtain an accredited professional architectural degree (B.Arch. or M.Arch.).

2. Complete a state-required minimum internship—usually three equivalent calendar years of architectural office experience.

3. Apply for and pass a state-administered architectural registration exam, following which the state issues a certificate of registration or license to practice architecture.

For most applicants, the examination itself represents the ordeal. Why the ordeal, and why bother testing architects who already have survived architectural school to get their professionally accredited diploma?

Architects are licensed because the design and construction of buildings are presumed to affect the health, safety, and welfare of the public. Under the federal Constitution, government is empowered to make laws regulating the actions and practices of individuals or institutions to protect the general public. The practice of architecture is no exception. The states want to ensure that anyone claiming to be an architect meets certain minimum qualifications concerning professional competency. Further, because of variability in educational standards, states have chosen to administer their own tests for competency. Therefore let us look at both the exam and qualifying for the exam.

A number of states have their own unique versions of what they actually consider to be three years of internship. Some states grant internship credit for time spent teaching, doing research, or conducting postprofessional degree studies in advanced graduate programs. Others are stricter, demanding that the three years be composed entirely of architectural design practice in the offices of licensed practicing architects. A state-by-state inquiry will reveal the qualification policy of each state. However, increasing numbers of states have adopted NCARB's Intern Development Program standards, making it easier for aspiring architects to understand what is needed to satisfy qualification requirements.

Over the years, the NCARB exam, adopted by most states as the standard registration exam, has been changed many times in both form and content. The NCARB, in its continuing efforts to improve the quality and reliability of its exam, has experimented with and used successive examination approaches that inevitably drew criticism from practitioners, teachers, and licensing candidates for various reasons: too long, too technical, too subjective, too ambiguous, too conceptual, too practical, too irrelevant, and . . . too easy or too hard. Indeed, since the first edition of this book was published in 1985, the NCARB examination format has changed several times. And no doubt a few years after this edition has appeared, the exam will have changed several more times. No matter when you take the exam, always obtain up-to-date qualification and testing information from the state where you are seeking registration.

NCARB's standardized examination is currently a multidivision Computerized Mastery Test (CMT). Developed by the Educational Testing Service in Princeton, New Jersey, the CMT for architectural registration is supposed to be the most efficient, most accurate, most reliable, fairest examination yet. It is designed to distinguish more clearly between candidates who pass and those who fail. It reportedly can make sharper distinctions because all questions have been pretested, are of average difficulty, and are not easily answered by guessing. Moreover, a candidate can attempt one, several, or all divisions of the examination throughout the year at one of the NCARB's many authorized, computer-based testing centers. (Formerly, the examination was given only once a year, which meant that some candidates needed several years to obtain their license.)

Each division of the exam contains several discrete sets of questions, with each set providing comprehensive coverage of the subject matter in the division. As candidates complete the initial question sets, the system monitors their answers. If a candidate clearly is passing or failing, the system stops administering that exam division. If a passing or failing pattern is not clear, the system continues with additional sets of questions for that division until a clear passing or failing pattern is detected. Thus candidates do not necessarily answer the same number of questions. Nor do candidates need to know much about computers, since the exam begins with a tutorial on how to use the mouse and manipulate icons on the monitor screen. However, the exam does require graphic as well as multiple-choice responses.

The examination has nine divisions:

1. Pre-Design
2. Site Planning (requires graphic solutions)
3. Building Planning (requires graphic solutions)
4. Building Technology (requires graphic solutions)
5. General Structures
6. Lateral Forces
7. Mechanical and Electrical Systems
8. Materials and Methods
9. Construction Documents and Services

As the list shows, the exam is broad in scope and places great emphasis on architectural technology as well as design. Examination candidates who qualify to take the exam usually study for it by enrolling in refresher seminars oriented toward the exam or by reviewing their own books, notes, and materials. Practice questions and graphic vignettes for the exam are available on disk or CD-ROM, and via the Internet. It is not uncommon for candidates to pass some divisions of the exam while failing others, and most states require reexamination for only those parts failed. Some states require that a candidate succeed in passing all divisions of the exam within some limited number of sittings; otherwise, he or she must retake the entire exam. The NCARB imposes no limit on the number of examination pass attempts.

Historically, the most commonly failed parts of the licensing exam have been the design portions. This may change with the now abandoned twelve-hour design problem, which was an exam tradition for many decades. Today's exam is intended not to ascertain aesthetic talent or presentation skills, but rather to test a candidate's ability to satisfy programmatic, organizational, building code, life safety, structural, and environmental requirements. As for other divisions, some candidates, perhaps shaky in handling quantitative problems, may struggle with the structural divisions. Good preparation is the key to winning the struggle.

Having passed the exam and become registered, an architect may legally offer architectural services to the public. States require that professionals periodically renew their licenses, but further examination is not required. A few states are considering imposing continuing education requirements as a condition for maintaining a license. Most states grant registration by reciprocity to architects licensed in other states, recognizing the equivalency of other states' licenses. NCARB issues a national certificate to applicants who have been licensed by NCARB examination in a state, and this certificate facilitates licensing in other states that use NCARB standards. For many architects the licensing exam has another significance: it may well be the last examination ever taken.

NCARB surveys of registered architects have shown that after licensing, more than 90 percent were in some form of architectural practice, with about 4 percent involved in teaching. Over half work in architectural firms with fewer than ten employees. By contrast, while a majority of the AIA's junior members are pursuing traditional architectural careers, roughly a quarter of them do not follow the school-internship-registration career path. Thus we can infer that although most licensed architects proceeded directly from school to practice, working primarily in small- to medium-sized firms, many graduate architects travel different routes or take side trips. Let us look at a few of these alternative routes.

Further Studies

Some architectural students, as they near the end of their primary architectural school education, desire further, more advanced schooling. Graduate architects also return to school to pursue new areas of interest after being in practice for several years. Among the reasons for such postprofessional degree graduate work are these:

• To gain new design experience in a specialized graduate program focused on topics such as urban design, housing, community planning and design, or computer-aided design.

• To study design with special teachers—mentors for young architects. Aware of and respectful of the work, methodology, and aesthetic philosophy of a particular professor at a particular school, graduate students can spend a year or more working with that professor, not necessarily to learn a particular skill or acquire specialized knowledge but rather to gain deeper insight into the professor's unique way of thinking and approaching design.

• To acquire greater expertise in architectural subspecialties, apart from design, such as history and theory, building technology, or construction management.

• To shift into fields closely related to architecture, such as landscape architecture, urban planning, interior design, or graphics.

• To change fields substantially, going from architecture to business, law, engineering, real estate finance, public administration, or even medicine.

Postprofessional degree study enhances your knowledge, capabilities, and career potential. In the competitive marketplace where professionals must survive, advanced degrees are clearly an asset, and they may be indispensable in some areas. For example, most universities will not appoint or promote faculty who do not hold the highest degree offered in the faculty appointee's field of study. Federal and local government agencies recognize advanced degrees in determining employees' salaries and positions. On the other hand, in traditional architectural practice, holding an advanced, postprofessional degree is much less critical to an architect's future; talent and personal characteristics are much more important. Statistically a small minority of all graduate architects pursue further graduate study after completion of architectural school and receipt of their first professional degree, whether a B.Arch or M.Arch.

If postprofessional studies are of interest and you are looking at various graduate schools, consider many of the same issues applicable to choosing a first professional degree program, described in the previous chapter. Also note that, in pursuing further studies in architectural design, you will receive a second, specialized master's degree, not a doctorate, since doctoral degrees generally are not awarded in the field of architectural design. Typically doctorates related to architecture are available only in architectural history and, at a few schools, architectural technology.

Continuing Education

Architects never stop learning, partly because there is so much to learn, but also because there is always new knowledge to be acquired: new design theories, new work methods, new management practices, new computer applications, new construction materials and techniques, new building codes and regulations. As in all other professions, architects have an obligation, to both clients and the public, to keep abreast of developing knowledge and evolving standards applicable to architectural practice. Consequently, architects continue pursuing education throughout their careers.

Continuing education can be structured and formalized, as it is in universities, with organized classes and instruction. Most structured, continuing education programs are sponsored by the American Institute of Architects (AIA), by some architecture schools, or by trade associations and professional organizations concerned with issues such as life safety, environmental protection, computers, building technology, and construction industry products. Or it can occur informally through the personal, ongoing efforts of the individual architect's continually reading articles in professional journals, studying technical literature, participating in seminars and conferences, or attending lectures.

To ensure that its members maintain and regularly update their practical knowledge, the AIA has adopted a continuing education system (CES). It requires members to verify their professional development by documenting continuing education "learning units" comprising a record of time, effort, and subject matter related to specific educational activities. The CES identifies critical areas for continuing education—for example, public health, safety, and welfare—but is nevertheless flexible, allowing each architect to select his or her own learning objectives. Some state registration boards also require evidence of continuing education for license renewal, and the AIA's goal is for all states to accept its CES transcript as sufficient proof.

Travel

No architect is ever fully educated until he or she has traveled beyond the borders of home territory. In particular, travel to Europe, from which so much of our Western architectural heritage derives, is a must-do—an educational experience not to be postponed. And if time and money permit, travel to more exotic parts of the world—Japan, India, the Middle East, North Africa, Latin America—is equally enlightening and stimulating. Fortunately, many architectural schools conduct study-abroad programs during summers and sometimes during regular school semesters, offering aspiring architects unique opportunities to see and study firsthand the towns, cities, and buildings known only from photographs and drawings in history books.

Any architect who has traveled will tell you that no amount of viewing slides or perusing books in the library can match educationally the experience of walking the streets of Rome, Paris, Istanbul, Beijing, or Kyoto. There is no substitute for analyzing, sketching, and photographing yourself the promenades, piazzas, villas, palaces, temples, churches, civic buildings, and marketplaces found on other continents. Touching architecture directly, from the most ancient to the most modern, is the only way truly to understand it. If you cannot travel while you are an architecture student, make sure you travel soon after finishing your studies, and continue to travel throughout your career.

In fact, American architects also should see as much of America as possible. Although much of our architectural heritage originated in Europe, there is a diverse American architectural heritage resulting from transplantation, reinterpretation, amalgamation, and invention of urban and architectural antecedents. Architects should see complex American cities like Boston, New York, Philadelphia, Washington, D.C., Miami, Chicago, and San Francisco. They should visit traditional towns like Charleston, South Carolina, Annapolis, Maryland, and urban settlements first laid out by the Spanish in the Southwest and Far West. Equally important, they should travel to sense fully the scale and diversity of the expansive

A travel sketch of Sienna's campanile and plaza (by Stanley I. Hallet).

North American landscape, to understand not only America's architecture but also how that architecture has been placed—sometimes well, sometimes badly—on the land.

Travel before settling down too permanently, since nothing impedes traveling like an excess of obligations at home, wherever that may be. Premature commitments to a job or practice, to a spouse, to children, or to a mortgage can make traveling difficult. Constrained vacation schedules, tight work schedules, financial limitations, and domestic entanglements can all get in the way of a summer in Europe or a year abroad.

Traditionally young architects have always traveled abroad to study the architectural and artistic heritages of other countries, making sketches of both humble and monumental environments. A young architect can even live and work abroad, absorbing far more of other cultures than is possible as a tourist. American architects continue to have such opportunities. They can seek overseas employment with either foreign or American architectural firms, which design increasing numbers of projects in Europe, Asia, Latin America, and Africa. They can work for government agencies or join the Peace Corps. They can compete for travel fellowships available to architects, mostly for European study and travel. Architects who teach can seek Fulbright lectureships and teaching exchange fellowships, which permit them to spend considerable time abroad. Regardless of the method by which you travel, it is an experience that forever influences your attitude as both architect and citizen. Time abroad broadens immeasurably.

Teaching

"Those who can, do—those who can't, teach!" So goes George Bernard Shaw's old saying. Although this may be partially true in some fields of education, it is less than appropriate when applied to teaching architecture, where many faculty both "teach" and "do" architecture.

Teaching architecture is an attractive career option for those so inclined and qualified. Universities require architectural design and technology faculty at least to have master's degrees. Architectural historians usually are expected to hold Ph.D. degrees. Most universities allow architecture faculty to consult and engage in private practice outside of school. Faculty who practice or consult can significantly augment their teaching income, and conversely, their steady teaching income makes it easier to begin and maintain practices, especially when economic circumstances in the construction marketplace are unfavorable. Although the academic salaries earned by teachers of architecture are modest compared to those in professions such as medicine, law, business, engineering, or computer sciences, they generally are comparable to salaries paid to professors in the arts and humanities. Perhaps most surprising, architecture professors' salaries can be comparable to the incomes of architects in full-time practice, particularly in smaller firms.

Many talented architectural graduates begin their teaching careers soon after completing advanced graduate studies. They may have already gained some teaching experience as graduate teaching assistants before finishing school, or they may have completed school and spent several years in practice. Initial appointments are at the level of instructor, lecturer, or assistant professor, and they may be adjunct, part-time appointments, made annually, or full-time, tenure-track appointments. The latter normally entail a multiyear, renewable contract. After a defined period, typically five or six years, a tenure-track assistant professor must be formally reviewed for tenure and promotion by both departmental and campus-wide tenure committees.

Tenure review encompasses evaluating three areas of achievement: teaching, research (or original creative work), and service to the university, the profession, and the public. Formal review for tenure leads to one of two outcomes: the university can grant the professor tenure, in effect guaranteeing permanent employment; or it can deny tenure, obliging the faculty member to leave after the following academic year. Clearly the tenure-granting process puts substantial pressure on architecture faculty to build their case over a relatively short period of time. Given the longer gestation period needed by architects, in comparison to mathematicians or historians, to establish themselves in the field, it is difficult for many architecture professors to qualify for tenure, no matter how talented they are.

Architecture schools prefer to hire new, young faculty for tenure-track positions who show both academic and professional promise through a combination of scholastic achievement and practical experience. Recruiting committees look for strong academic records, compelling portfolios showing work independently designed or built, awards for work or work exhibited, documented original research, articles written and published, participation in design competitions and scholarly conferences, outstanding references, and evidence of teaching ability. Some schools will not hire architectural faculty to teach design unless they are licensed. On the other hand, most schools encourage young design faculty to become licensed and pursue professional practice, or to undertake research and scholarship, in addition to their academic obligations. It is well understood that getting tenure depends as much on a record of demonstrated excellence in research, publication, and design as it does on teaching excellence.

Despite tenure pressures, teaching offers many significant benefits, not the least of which is the intellectual discourse and stimulation it provides. Faculty are continually challenged by students and colleagues. New ideas and information flow readily back and forth, not only between academics but also between academics and practitioners. Teaching allows time and opportunity for research, theoretical speculation and exploration, and writing. Good teachers act as exchangers, bringing their research and practice into their teaching and their teaching into their research and practice. And, of course, teaching is its own reward, offering the great satisfaction of seeing students learning, discovering, creating, and growing, in part due to the efforts of their teachers.

The drawbacks to teaching are predictable: inadequate compensation in the absence of supplemental income, especially affecting professors who have families but are not practicing architects; the demands of seeking tenure, and not getting it; the administrative complexities, inefficiencies, and breakdowns endemic to universities;

the potential for boredom arising from too many repetitions of courses and subject matter, which in turn can bore students; intellectual stagnation arising from insufficient activity outside the classroom or studio, a commonly encountered condition with teachers who do nothing but teach or have been teaching the same material for too long. Most of these drawbacks, however, are adequately offset by the positive benefits or avoided altogether through the efforts of helpful colleagues, wise mentors, and sensitive administrators.

Work in Related Fields

Throughout this book, "practicing architecture" refers to professionals directly responsible for the aesthetic, functional, and technical design of buildings. Design is the core subject in almost every architectural school, the core topic of almost every architectural magazine. Yet many would-be architects discover, either during or after graduation from architectural school, that design per se and traditional architectural practice are not their cup of tea. They may come to this conclusion because of a perceived lack of talent, lack of interest and motivation, newly discovered interests, or a desire to make more money or have more power.

But they also may realize that architectural education, with its unique curriculum and approach, has prepared them well for other endeavors. Consider the breadth of subjects studied: drawing and graphics; math, science, and engineering; computers; management; history; humanities and social studies; and, above all, design, that most complex and integrative of activities demanding research and analysis, critical thinking, imagination, conflict resolution, and constructive synthesis. Architecture students, regardless of their talent, learn how to work hard, to reason, to organize and to synthesize, invaluable skills in almost any field. Therefore, no matter what leads them away from architectural design, graduate architects enjoy numerous career choices that capitalize on their architectural education.

Landscape architecture, urban planning, historic preservation, and interior design are the most closely related fields because they all touch directly on the design and protection of physical environments. All four of these alternative fields intersect with architectural design. They share methods and tools, common cultural histories, and similar aesthetic and functional goals. All involve construction technology. Further, their territories undeniably overlap: landscapes encompass cities, which in turn encompass landscapes and buildings, which encompass interiors. Like architecture, each of these allied professions has its own educational prerequisites and its own body of theory, readily appreciated and mastered by someone trained in architecture. Not surprisingly, many landscape architects, urban planners, historic preservationists, and interior designers studied architecture first.

Related less closely in methodology and goals, but powerfully affecting the design of the built environment, are the building development fields: construction contracting and management, and real estate development, financing, and marketing. These are not design professions, nor are they constituent parts of architectural practice, but architecture, viewed as a business product and treated as real estate, is their concern.

Construction contractors construct buildings, purchasing and assembling the labor and materials needed and coordinating the work of subcontractors and suppliers. They are expected to follow drawings and specifications prepared by architects. But architects, like contractors, work for building owners or developers. The latter identify markets, generate programs and operational concepts, acquire property, obtain financing, hire the design team, negotiate contracts with construction contractors, and then lease, sell, or occupy the improved property. Owners and developers, not architects, usually call the shots, along with investors, lenders, bankers, and brokers who provide the funds for purchasing or developing real estate. Thus graduate architects occasionally enter these fields, having discovered that, first, they often have more control over the development process, and, second, that financing buildings can be much more economically rewarding than designing them, if not as much fun.

Structural and civil engineering are also related to architecture, although far more engineers leave engineering for architecture than the reverse. It is rare to find licensed, practicing engineers who also hold architectural degrees, but some architects have earned engineering degrees before studying architecture. Architects, with their mathematical aptitude and analytical approach to design, could be good engineers, but they may be deterred for psychological and social reasons, since engineers are considered less artistic and more narrowly focused than architects. Also considerable additional time in school is needed to earn engineering credentials.

Finally, many architects are drawn into government service and public administration. Federal, state, county, and municipal governments are responsible for a great amount of real estate, some of which they create, but most of which they manage or regulate. This includes all types of facilities, from national parks and military bases to office buildings and housing. Architects have a vital role to play within government at all levels, overseeing this vast network of property and, equally important, ensuring that proposed new construction is well designed.

Sometimes architects in the public sector act as initiators and designers, developing proposals and design concepts. Government architects may even prepare detailed construction drawings and specifications for projects. More often they act as reviewers, regulators, or project managers, overseeing design and construction activities performed by outside contractors or consulting architectural firms. Or they may become managers of governmental bureaus, divisions, or departments concerned with more general policies and procedures rather than specific projects or properties. Occasionally one hears of architects' becoming politicians, running for office, and winning elections. They no longer practice architecture, but architects in government may have opportunities to make decisions that have profound impact on architects or architecture, especially when they assume the role of client.

Architects in government may miss out on the highs and lows of practice, the joys or sorrows of self-employment and self-expression.

They certainly will not get rich, but they do enjoy the benefits of stable, steady employment, paid vacations, insurance and health programs, and sometimes important policymaking responsibilities.

Abandoning Architecture

Lovely as it is, costly as it was, architecture is regrettably abandoned by a number of graduate architects, usually for one or more of the reasons specified earlier. They also may abandon the field out of disillusionment or frustration. They might go back to school and study law or business, sell insurance or lumber, or drop out entirely to spend their time sailing in the South Pacific. In almost all cases, the benefits of architecture were felt to be insufficient to justify the burdens.

It would be interesting to compile and compare abandonment statistics for diverse professions. I suspect that architecture would be high on the list, like many nonprofessional liberal arts fields pursued enthusiastically by students, only to be abandoned later under marketplace or other pressures. The laws of supply and demand certainly contribute to the abandonment impulse in architecture, with more and more architects competing for less and less work when times are bad. However, those who completely leave architecture probably do so with mixed feelings and a sense of loss.

Recalling the external impediments and inequities that architects know to be real, often inescapable, and beyond control makes it easier to deal with and rationalize such feelings. But the feelings of lost opportunity, unused creativity, and unrealized aspirations must be harder to deal with. The intellectual and emotional payoffs of design exploration and invention, the fun of building, the delights of visual composition, of space and form: these are the potential rewards left behind that few other careers can provide.

III

Being an Architect

8

The Building Process and the Architect's Role

The regulated profession of architecture is relatively new, yet there have been architects for as long as societies have built, with little distinction between designers and builders. In ancient, traditional cultures and languages, the same word was used for both architect and builder. Construction was an integrated craft in which the master mason or master carpenter knew how to design, assemble labor and materials, estimate costs, manage the construction process, and erect structures from foundation to roof. Thus the first people to provide shelter for themselves or for others became, in essence, the first architects. Traditionally an architect was anyone with the ability to conceptualize, describe geometry, draw, and construct without subsequent collapse.

The industrial revolution changed the craft of building. The advent of new materials, new machines, new engineering techniques, and new building requirements made it increasingly difficult for any one person or organization to master every facet of building design and construction. Specialization became inevitable. New and technically complex structural systems demanded expertise beyond that of a master mason or master carpenter. The proliferation of highly specialized subcontractors redefined the role of the general contractor, whose own labor force built less and less of the building. The complexities of construction increasingly became matters for experts who would complement the efforts of the architect.

Architecture became a legitimate, professional discipline. The first school of architecture in the United States was established at the Massachusetts Institute of Technology in 1868, and architecture was soon recognized as a learned and governable profession as the various states enacted legislation for the licensing of architects. In the twentieth century, the practicing architect's territory has become increasingly circumscribed, limited primarily to the provision of building design services in conjunction with the engineering services provided by structural, mechanical, electrical, and civil engineers.

The conventionally defined role of architects in society appears to be well understood. Architects are both technologists and artists whose design talents yield buildings with beauty, stability, utility,

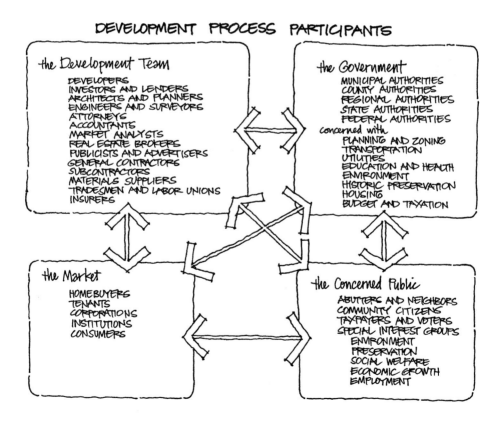

and, it is often hoped, cost-effectiveness. Architects' functional and legal responsibility is to prepare drawings and specifications accurately showing what to construct, to assist clients in getting project designs approved by all concerned parties, and to mediate and provide guidance during the construction of projects. The successful architect must have extensive technical and engineering knowledge, organizational and managerial ability, sociological and political sensitivity, legal acumen, selling and marketing skills, economic and accounting know-how, social and business connections, and some financial resources, not to mention design talent and a commitment to hard work.

Nevertheless, this all sounds rather generalized, not specialized. If the architect is obliged to be so professionally ambidextrous, why do architects not continue to be traditional master builders? The answer is best given by exploring the process through which buildings are created and identifying all of the participants in that process. Then the architect's role will be clear and comprehensible—at least the role of those architects who choose to practice architecture, the art and science of building design.

How Projects Get Built

Need

"Necessity is the mother of invention," another old saw, does a good job of telling us why most building projects get started. Someone must believe that there is an unmet need, either existing or future. Economists would describe it as identification of a market, or market demand. Sociologists and anthropologists would characterize it as need deriving from more basic human motivations and activities. Some see such needs as problems to be solved, or as opportunities for profit, or as ways to serve humankind. In all cases, no project will come to life unless some number of people, perhaps with differing perceptions and goals, agree that there is a genuine need for whatever is to be built.

In architectural parlance, project needs are usually expressed as a "program" or "brief." The program document embodies in detail specific project objectives and requirements that, if met, will adequately satisfy the basic need. Thus a well-written program generally includes a thorough description of functional, aesthetic, social, cultural, and other aspirations; a list of operational activities to be accommodated and their functional interrelationships; an associated menu of spaces and related floor area requirements (measured in square feet or square meters); special technical or equipment requirements; and any other stipulations affecting the project's design.

Once the project need is recognized and verified and the program is established, then the process of meeting the need can commence in earnest. The accompanying diagram illustrates this building process, but not from the point of view of the architect. Instead, it shows the process from a position of neutrality, giving no special weight to any particular segment. It is a somewhat simplified, though comprehensive, diagram, which includes steps that may be inapplicable to certain kinds of projects. It also does not show time and activity durations in a necessarily proportional way, since these vary widely from project to project. The important dimensions of the diagram are the number and interrelationship of activities.

Site

Along with recognition of project need comes the necessity for a place to meet the need—a site. Few projects can be contemplated without a place to put them. In fact, sometimes the site is available before the need to improve it is felt. Whoever undertakes the development of the project—the owner, developer, or entrepreneur client in our model—must eventually have control of a site, either by owning it or leasing it from someone else. With some projects, the architect's client may have owned the project site for a long time, but for many others, the client may be acquiring the site, be it a small lot, an old building to be remodeled, or a parcel containing hundreds of acres.

With project need and site identified, the owner/client must then assemble the resources and expertise required to transform ideas into reality. The essential resource is of course money to pay for all

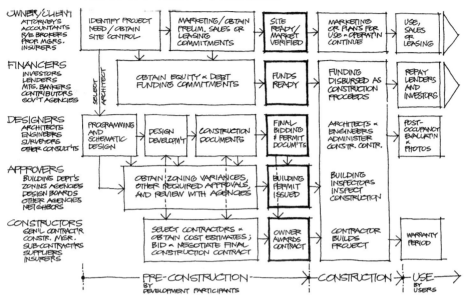

THE DEVELOPMENT PROCESS

of the costs incurred in project development—property acquisition costs, architectural and engineering fees, legal fees, project administration costs, market analysis costs, financing fees and interest on debt, accounting fees, advertising and public relations expenses, selling and leasing costs, insurance premiums, zoning and building permit process costs, and direct construction costs for all the labor, material, and equipment needed to build. Most of these expenses will be incurred for any project, from building a house to building a new city.

Financing

A critical piece of the development puzzle is financing, without which nothing can be built. There are basically two types of financing: equity funding and debt funding. Equity funding represents at-risk monies that the owner/client invests out of pocket or from the pockets of partners, stockholders, or contributors. If an income-producing project fails, the equity invested may never be recovered.

Debt funding represents monies that are borrowed by the owner/client with a legal obligation to repay, usually with interest, within some specified period of time. The lender of such funds makes a loan evidenced by some form of note, or IOU, signed by the borrower. There are many sources of debt financing. Institutions that directly make loans for real estate development include commercial banks, savings and loan associations, insurance companies, pension funds, investment trusts, and some credit unions. Loans may also be obtained through mortgage bankers, who act as intermediaries between lenders and borrowers. Federal, state, city, and county governments sometimes make loans for special kinds of projects that are deemed to be in the public interest, such as low-income housing or job-creating industrial facilities.

Sometimes the public lends money directly to government agencies by purchasing bonds, which are government IOUs issued to finance public projects such as schools, hospitals, or transportation facilities. Ultimately the public supplies the money for all construction, private or governmental. Most of the funds that lending institutions make available for real estate loans come from savers' deposits entrusted to such institutions by individuals. If people did not save, there would be no pool of capital available for debt financing, and very little construction would occur because the majority of monies invested in construction and property acquisition is borrowed. Indeed, in developing privately financed real estate, only 25 to 30 percent of the costs of a project are paid for with equity funds. Thus the availability and cost of credit in our economic system is inexorably linked to the building process and the welfare of many architects.

Not all projects depend directly on the credit market for capital. Most nonprofit museums, performing arts centers, government and other civic buildings, religious structures, and public education facilities are built with funds raised through donations, grants, sale of marketable assets, or budgetary appropriations. Their funding is, in effect, entirely composed of equity, with no mortgage financing required.

Design and Design Approvals

As the owner/client wrestles with the intricacies of raising capital for building, architects and engineers must develop basic design strategies for executing the project. This phase of work is crucial; it establishes the fundamental concept for the design, taking into account hundreds of potentially conflicting factors: detailed program requirements, site conditions, construction budget constraints, and regulatory criteria embodied in zoning ordinances, environmental regulations, and building codes—not to mention the aesthetic idiosyncrasies of both architect and client. The type of

uses, densities, and overall building configurations legally permitted on any given urban or suburban site must be approved by seemingly countless agencies of government and citizens' groups with jurisdiction over the project, and this takes substantial amounts of time, patience, dialogue, persuasion, and sensitivity. In many counties and municipalities, there can be several review boards, in addition to the building permit department, that must approve development proposals prior to construction. Each reviewing authority may have its own, separate design criteria and may require several interim reviews.

Usually, seeking such approvals, along with providing appropriate design advice, is carried out as a team effort, the team typically consisting of the designers, the client, possibly the client's attorney, and other expert consultants, such as civil and transportation engineers, economic analysts, and environmental scientists. It is not unusual for such efforts to be delayed in cases where proposed development is controversial; many projects rest quietly unrealized in the file drawers of architectural offices.

Engineers and Other Design Consultants

Engineers play a critical part in the building process. Structural engineers analyze the load-bearing portions of buildings—the skeleton or frame, along with floors, roofs, and walls—and specify the sizes, dimensions, types of material, and details of connection for all such systems or components after the architect generally determines the overall geometry of the building. In similar fashion, mechanical and electrical engineers are responsible for analyzing and designing heating, air-conditioning, ventilating, plumbing, and electrical distribution systems. They too cannot undertake their work until the architect has provided a preliminary design that approximates the intended, final architectural product.

Civil engineers undertake the design of site grading, roadways, storm water management systems, water supply and sanitary sewer systems, bridges, and other site utilities or structures. Their engineering design work also cannot begin until the architect has prepared a preliminary site plan showing the proposed location and shape of buildings. Architects, in turn, must base their initial site planning on topographic and site boundary surveys provided by licensed land surveyors, who are often employed by civil engineers. In the case of residential and industrial subdivisions, civil engineers, rather than architects or landscape architects, sometimes prepare the preliminary site plans from which the final engineering will proceed.

Other specialized engineering expertise may be needed to supplement normal structural, mechanical, electrical, and civil engineering services. Projects such as theaters, churches, schools, hotels, hospitals, embassies, museums, and, occasionally, houses can pose unique technical problems ranging from lighting to acoustics to specialized food service operations. Acoustical engineers are concerned with the control of sound—its transmission, reflection, and absorption. Lighting consultants are concerned with illuminating interior and exterior environments, using both daylight and electric lighting. They focus on the aesthetic quality of light as well as the selection and placement of lighting for adequate task illumination. There are theater consultants, kitchen consultants, health care design consultants, security consultants, and exhibition and graphics consultants. Whatever the project, it is generally the architect's responsibility first to select, then to coordinate, the efforts of such disparate design consultants.

Another consultant often engaged by the architect or client is the landscape architect. Although some landscape architects deal mostly with large-scale land planning (urban and suburban master plans, residential subdivision layouts, design of parks and roadways), potentially overlapping with civil engineers and architects, many continue to practice design at the smaller, more horticulturally oriented scale of garden and building site design. The latter concentrate on the selection, layout, installation, and maintenance of plant materials (trees, shrubs, and ground covers). The building architect may call on the landscape consultant to provide a complete landscape plan or only to advise about basic plant material selection. Very few architects are sufficiently knowledgeable about horticulture and local ecology to assume this responsibility, although they may be competent to make basic decisions about plant type and layout.

Finally comes the interior designer or decorator, with whom there is perhaps the greatest potential overlap and conflict from the architect's point of view. Hardly an architect breathes who does not consider himself or herself to be a qualified interior designer. (Some architects refer to interior "desecrators.") It is usually the client, not the architect, who decides to hire an interior designer or decorator to assume responsibility for interior furniture and furnishings. What makes life difficult for all parties is that it can be unclear where architectural design stops and interior design begins. It is also a lopsided struggle, since architects are confident that they can do interiors and that interior decorators cannot do architecture. Nevertheless, fruitful collaborations occur.

In residential and commercial projects, interior designers, if employed, help the owner select furniture and upholstery, carpeting, paint colors, wall coverings, window treatments, lamps, decorative accessories, and occasionally artwork. The architect's work may not go beyond shaping spaces to contain, and serve as background for, the interior designer's layers of decor. Like any other consultant group there are both good and bad interior designers, some of whom are also architects. For the sensitive and motivated architect, the best tactic is to design interior spaces that are visually compelling and resistant to decorative excess and then to persuade the client to consider the interiors an integral part of the architecture, so that the client decides that the best interior design consultant is in fact the architect.

You might now be wondering about the legal and financial relationships of expert consultants to the architect and other participants in the building process. Most expert participants operate as independent consultants, retained either by the architect as subcontractors or by the owner/client. Consultants hired by the architect are responsible to and compensated by the architect. This relationship gives the architect more control over the actions and decisions of such consultants, since the consultants must rely on the architect not only for direction but also for payment of their fees, a situation in which the architect clearly has real leverage.

On the other hand, the architect assumes legal and financial responsibility for the work performed by such consultants since, from the client's point of view, the architect is furnishing the services, there being no direct relationship between the client and the consultant. Further the architect, not the client, must pay for the consultant's services, and unless the consultant agrees otherwise, the architect is obligated to compensate the consultant even if the client fails to compensate the architect. Prudent architects usually insist that payment by the architect to the consultant be contingent on payment by the client to the architect.

When consultants work directly for the client, the architect may lose some control over what the consultant does, but only if such control is voluntarily relinquished. If the architect resists abdicating and can establish a positive working relationship among all parties, this form of contractual relationship can be advantageous to everyone. The architect is better off because he or she does not assume the responsibility, legally or financially, for the work of other experts—work that the architect is usually not qualified to perform—and the consultants' fees are paid directly by the client without going through the architect. Nevertheless, under either arrangement, it is usually the architect's job to act as coordinator for all design services.

Some design firms offer a combination of architectural and engineering (A/E) services. Indeed, a few, very large A/E firms design a majority of all construction built in the United States, partly because of their multidisciplinary service approach. Under one organizational umbrella are architects, landscape architects, planners, interior designers, structural engineers, mechanical and electrical engineers, civil engineers, and construction cost estimators. These groups of in-house experts play their respective roles as if they were independent professional consulting firms sharing a single office space. Because these experts all work for one firm, coordination and communication are facilitated although internal disputes and struggles for power may arise. Nevertheless, to clients, it is the equivalent of one-stop shopping for building design services. Some of these firms have reached even further, offering construction management, market analysis, and real estate project feasibility services along with comprehensive A/E design services. The only thing they do not offer the client is financing.

Brokers

Several types of brokers—go-betweens who help buyers find sellers or, more usually, sellers find buyers—may be involved in development. Mortgage loan brokers help buyers of money—borrowers—find sellers of money—lenders. Real estate brokers help property owners sell property, or they may assist developers in finding and acquiring property for development. Other real estate specialists concentrate on leasing, putting together landlords (lessors) and tenants (lessees), and some assist owners of leased property in managing such property.

All brokers and property managers earn fees for their services, usually a percentage of the selling price or rents received. Architects are frequently surprised, and chagrined, by brokers' fees, which can significantly exceed architects' fees in a given project for what appears to be significantly less work, less difficult work, and much less financial risk. This differential reflects the relative market value our economic system places on each service, not necessarily the cost of the service, so be forewarned.

Attorneys

Some projects are legally complex, frequently because of ownership, financing, or regulatory complexities. From the owner/client's viewpoint, an array of legal relationships, each defined by a written or verbal contract, complicates the process but also helps attorneys earn a living. Attorneys are hired by owner/clients to provide legal advice and to cope with these legal complexities throughout each step of project development. Some attorneys are very effective, serving as deal makers, whereas others can impede progress, turning into deal breakers. Inevitably architects have to cope with somebody's lawyer, if not their own.

Construction Contractors

Of all the relationships and contracts mentioned, none is as critical to project realization as those between owner/client and general contractor. Construction contracts are the single largest category of development expense. Direct construction costs, along with land costs and loan interest, can account for over 90 percent of total development expenses, with the balance composed of professional and other fees, taxes, insurance, marketing, and administrative overhead.

The role of the construction contractor is paramount, not only because this is the most costly contract, but also because the efficacy and quality of construction have great impact on the economic, technical, and aesthetic outcome of the project. Architects are very concerned with construction and those who perform it, since the realization of their design and their client's satisfaction depend substantially on how well builders build.

Except for very small projects, such as enclosing a screen porch or building a patio, more than one contractor will be required to complete most construction work. Specialization has been taken to its limit in the construction industry. Virtually no general contractor in existence can perform all of the tasks required to build a project, even a modest one. Thus general contractors depend on a collection of independent subcontractors to perform specific pieces or phases of the construction work. Further, they depend on dozens of separate suppliers to furnish hundreds of different materials and equipment items that go into the simplest of projects.

For example, to build a house, a general contractor would depend on the following subcontractors, labor trade specialties, and suppliers to execute an architect's design. (This list assumes that the general contractor has its own supervisory, carpentry, and unskilled labor force):

Site clearing and excavation

Site utilities

Masonry

Plumbing

Heating and air-conditioning

Lumber and millwork

Doors and windows

Concrete

Glass and glazing

Roofing

Electrical

Lighting fixtures

Drywall and plaster

Painting

Tile work

Flooring

Paving

Landscaping

For more complex structures such as office buildings, schools, or hospitals, additional listees include:

Steel mills, shop fabricators, and erectors

Curtain walls

Elevators and escalators

Suppliers of miscellaneous specialties

Foundation sheeting and shoring

Concrete precasters

General contracting is a brokering operation. A contractor takes the architects' and engineers' drawings and specifications, studies them, distributes them to prospective subcontractors and suppliers, and then obtains cost estimates and bids for furnishing and installing every component of the project. To this sum of labor and material costs, the general contractor adds a fee for overhead and profit.

In some projects the contractor is selected during the early design phases, working closely with the architect and owner/client to monitor probable construction costs, and a final construction contract is negotiated as detailed drawings are completed. This process can save time, and potentially money, since the contractor participates in making cost-affecting design decisions. Many times, however, it is in the owner/client's interest to solicit competitive bids from several general contractors. Although this process takes more time than the negotiated contract approach, it can yield the lowest price if contractors are reasonably competitive and anxious to bid. Prudent owners and architects normally award the contract to the lowest bidder who is financially and technically qualified.

Once a contract is signed, the general contractor orders and purchases the needed materials, executes subcontracts, organizes and coordinates suppliers and subcontractors, and, in effect, sells the project to the owner/client at a marked-up price. Construction is supposed to be carried out in strict accordance with the architect's plans as approved by the owner/client and by government agencies and lending institutions. However, general contractors, like every subcontractor and supplier, have one primary business motive: to make a profit. Therefore their goal is to buy low and sell high, putting them into periodic conflict with the architect and owner/client, since the latter's objective, among others, is to get the most for the money from the contractor. This explains why project owners, architects, and contractors are usually separate entities linked together by contractual agreements, with the architect being primarily responsible for protecting the client's interest while simultaneously being fair to the contractor. In fact during construction, the architect has an obligation to resolve disputes objectively between owner and contractor, even if it means siding with the contractor.

Occasionally an owner/client will decide to hire a construction manager (CM) instead of a general contractor. A CM acts as a consultant, performing essentially the same bidding, supervisory, and coordination functions as a general contractor, but without having to deliver the project under a single contract for a single price. As an agent, the CM negotiates on behalf of the owner/client and enters into dozens of separate contracts with all the subcontractors and suppliers. This relationship does not always prove favorable for either the owner/client or the architect. With so many contracts to administer, the management and accounting burden is much greater, and the architect is often forced to spend excessive amounts of time on coordination and documentation during construction. Further, since there is no general contractor with overall project responsibility, it is easier for items to fall through the cracks of responsibility between subcontractors.

Role Playing

Different roles in the building process may be played by a single individual or entity. For example, an architect's client can act as general contractor. Large developers who build housing or commercial projects may have their own construction contracting department, design department, financing brokerage, real estate brokerage, property management department, or accounting and legal staffs under one corporate roof. Other developers are literally one-person operations, requiring only a telephone line, a computer, a fax machine, a long list of loyal subcontractors, suppliers, and consultants, and frequently minimal working capital (but lots of borrowing potential).

Similarly architects may step out of their design role by buying property, raising money, constructing or renovating buildings, and then selling or leasing them for a profit (or loss). Again, like the big corporate entrepreneur, the architect can assume the roles of developer and borrower, contractor, marketer, and investor, as well as designer. Nevertheless, each separate role must be played, each demands certain, distinguishable knowledge and actions, and each may draw on widely divergent talents or capabilities in the person assuming the roles. Note also that conflicts of interest can occur in playing multiple roles, the most problematic arising when architects act as general contractors for their clients. This was once considered unethical by the AIA, but no longer, the theory being that adequate disclosure of financial interests by the architect to the client somehow eliminates the presumed conflict of interest.

Project construction cannot begin until all of the proverbial ducks are in a row. Adequate funds must be secured and ready to flow; property control or ownership must be finalized; architectural and engineering design documents must be completed and approved

by all authorities; building permits must be issued; construction bids must have been obtained and contracts negotiated and signed; insurance must be in force; preliminary leasing or sales commitments must be in hand or market demand verified; and other minor though essential tasks must be finished. Unless all of these preconstruction necessities are checked off, the project cannot proceed. It is not uncommon for the development process to reach the point of construction commencement only to be stopped, sometimes forever, because one of these contingent necessities remains unsatisfied. Ask any architect, and you can see file drawers with completely drawn projects that went unbuilt because financing fell through, or zoning variances were denied, or title to the property became clouded, or citizen-sponsored lawsuits tied up the developer for years beyond the time when the project had been feasible.

Once a project begins, the construction period can last for months or years, depending on its size and complexity. House remodelings are notorious for taking as long to complete as new homes or office buildings. Delays are the norm, resulting from labor strikes, material and labor shortages, bad weather, unforeseen soil conditions, errors or changes in design, or poor construction planning. Some projects seem to be under construction forever (hospitals, college campuses, transportation terminals). During construction, the architect's role changes from design to design clarification and modification (known as change orders), coupled with periodic observation of the contractor's work. The architect continues to interact with the property owner, tenants, leasing agents, lenders, and inspectors having jurisdiction over the project.

Users and the Community

Users may never have a contract with any of the participants in the development process, but they are very real clients to the architect. They are the ultimate consumers of architecture, the community of people who finally see, touch, occupy, live in, and move through the finished product. Included are neighbors and those who work in buildings, visit them, or shop in them. They are the collective constituency of those involved directly in the building process. Building codes and zoning regulations protect them, not the architect, owner, contractor, or lenders.

It is therefore incumbent on the architect always to be aware of an invisible, nonpaying client sitting at the conference table whose interests must be duly represented and advocated by the architect. Neglected users or slighted community citizens can find recourse as if there had been a contract. They can organize protests, generate negative publicity, withhold rent, even file lawsuits and claims against everyone in sight, blaming the architect as well as the owner and contractor. Never forget or shortchange the user in particular and the public in general. And when possible, include representative users and concerned neighbors at the design conference table.

9

How Architects Work

Article 1 of the old AIA standard agreement between owner/client and architect (AIA Document B141) describes the architect's services and responsibilities, which are briefly summarized below. As you will see, the contract does two things at once. First, it says *what* the architect is going to do. Second, through well-chosen words and ordering of paragraphs, it suggests *how* the architect will perform the services. Theoretically such a description of services should tell us what we want to know about the work architects do. In this, the AIA document fails. But it does provide an outline we can fruitfully flesh out.

Basic architectural services consist of five phases, and the architect's work product is indicated for each phase:

Phase	Work product
1. Schematic design—analysis of the owner's program, site, and budget; preliminary design studies in sketch form and a preliminary estimate of probable construction cost.	Program diagrams Function diagrams Site plans, floor plans, sections, elevations, perspectives, models, in sketch form
2. Design development—further development of the schematic design; definition of basic project systems and materials; decision on project size, dimensions, architectural character; update estimate.	More precise plans, sections, elevations, site plan drawings; more realistic perspectives and study models constructed either manually or by computer

3. Construction documents—detailed design of the project, including all engineering design, selection of materials, establishment of dimensions, construction assembly details, appropriate construction notes (required to obtain construction bids and building permits).

Working drawings

Specifications

Bidding information

4. Bidding or negotiation—during or after completion of the construction documents, assisting the client in finding, screening, selecting qualified general contractors from whom bids may be obtained or with whom a contract may be negotiated; assisting the client in reviewing bids and awarding contracts.

Contractor's bids

Construction contracts

Modified design documents to meet budget limits

5. Construction administration—representing or assisting the client in administering the construction contract, including making design changes, site visits, reviewing the contractor's work, requests for payment, selecting colors and previously unspecified items, checking shop drawings prepared by fabricators, mediating disputes between contractor and owner.

Design clarification documents

Change orders

Field reports of site visits

Certifications for payment and completion

Beyond these five phases, the AIA contract goes on to describe so-called additional services that may be provided if the client wishes and the architect agrees. Otherwise they are normally excluded from basic services. These additional services can include economic feasibility studies, detailed cost estimates, interior design (for furniture and furnishings), surveying and measuring existing structures, special design or engineering consultation not usually required, and a host of other extras, all of which constitute, in the judgment of those signing the agreement, work beyond the scope anticipated for typical architectural design work.

This outline of services is more or less chronological, proceeding from the initial conceptual studies of design possibilities, the exploration of architectural ideas, to the more exact delineation and explication of what is to be built, and then finally to the execution of the project itself. This, for the most part, is what practicing architects do and, in the most general way, how they do it.

But let us probe further. This definition of work scope hardly tells us what happens in an architect's office on an hourly, daily, weekly, or even continuing basis to effectuate services and fulfill the

Table 9.1
Day-to-day tasks in architectural practice

| | Type of activities involved | | | | |
Primary job functions	Draw	Write	Read	Talk	Calculate
Running the office					
Client relations	0	+++	+	+++	0
Marketing and promotion	+	+++	++	+++	0
Firm management	0	++	++	+++	+++
Designing projects					
Project management	0	++	+	++	++
Programming and research	0	++	+++	+	++
Conceptual design	+++	0	+	+	+
Working drawings	+++	0	+	+	+
Specifications	0	+++	+++	+	0
Consultant coordination	0	+++	+++	++	0
Cost analysis	0	+	+++	++	+++
Executing projects					
Bidding and negotiation	0	++	++	+++	+++
Construction administration (office)	++	+++	++	++	+++
Construction administration (field)	0	+	0	+++	0

Note: 0 = almost none required, + = small amount required, + + = moderate amount required, + + + = great amount required.

architect's mission. Nor does it address how architectural offices are structured and operated.

To understand the nature of architectural practice, we must consider the specific acts that are common to all architectural organizations, small or large, private or governmental, domestic or foreign. Making use of descriptions found in various surveys conducted by the AIA, NCARB, and others, table 9.1 shows the many ongoing, primary job functions characterizing architectural practice. The activity classifications need some additional clarification before you can fully appreciate the significance of this chart.

Drawing

"Drawing" really refers to graphic forms of representation, whether produced manually or by computer. There are several different kinds of architectural drawings, of which some are particular to each phase of service. During the schematic design phase, most drawing is done manually. It is sketchy, quick, diagrammatic, at times impressionistic. Soft pencils, marking pens, charcoal, chalk, or colored pencils are used freely, along with inexpensive rolls of thin yellow or white tracing paper, which allows overlays of previous drawings to be made readily. Among the designer's primary tools at this point is the architectural scale for measuring dimensions. If one had to choose only three things essential to designing a work of architecture, they would be pencil, paper, and scale. Even when searching for concepts and exploring ideas, good designers regularly draw sketches to scale.

During the schematic design phase, good architects also make simple, conceptual, small-scale study models fashioned quickly out of cardboard, wood, plastic foam, or clay. These tiny models, perhaps only inches high, nevertheless can convey abstractly the overall compositional idea for a project.

After schematic design comes design development, and the architects' drawings become less sketchy and more precise, enlarging in scale. In addition to scales, pencils, and paper, designers working manually employ parallel bars or T-squares on drawing boards,

BEGIN:

RESEARCH & ANALYSIS OF PROJECT SITE, CLIENT, PROGRAM, BUDGET, REGULATIONS, HISTORICAL PRECEDENT

PROGRAM: A SCHOOL

SPACE/ACTIVITY	AREA	SPECIAL REQ'TS
CLASSROOMS	8 @ 900 SF	FLEXIBLE, BRIGHT..........
MUSIC STUDIO	1 @ 900 SF	ACOUSTIC, NEAR ART.....
ART STUDIO	1 @ 1200 SF	SKYLIGHT, TACKBOARD.....
CAFETERIA	3000 SF	STAGE, VENTILATION......
ADMINISTRATION	1500 SF	NEAR ENTRY, SECURE...
RESTROOMS	4 @ 400 SF	ALL TILE, WINDOWS.......
STORAGE	1000 SF	DISTRIBUTE AMONG......
MECHANICAL	1200 SF	FAR FROM MUSIC..........

SCHEMATIC DESIGN

CONCEPTUAL DIAGRAMS:
- SITE CONCEPTS
- VOLUMETRIC CONCEPTS
- PLAN & SECTION CONCEPTS
- IMAGE/FAÇADE CONCEPTS
- FUNCTIONAL LAYOUTS

INCREASE SCALE

ALTERNATE A ALTERNATE B ALTERNATE C ALTERNATE D ALTERNATE E ALTE[RNATE] F

SKETCHES OF BASIC CONCEPTUAL DESIGN:
- SITE PLAN
- FLOOR PLANS
- SECTIONS
- ELEVATIONS
- PERSPECTIVES, AXONS

INCREASE SCALE

ALTERNATE M

DESIGN DEVELOPMENT

ACCURATE DRAWINGS OF FINAL DESIGN
- SITE PLAN
- FLOOR PLANS
- SECTIONS
- ELEVATIONS
- PERSPECTIVES
- AXONOMETRICS
- TYPICAL WALL SECTIONS
- STRUCTURAL/MECH SCHEMA

INCREASE SCALE

DETAILED DRAFTING

WORKING DRAWINGS

FACE BRICK
CONC. BLOCK BACK-UP
1" CAVITY
2" RIGID INSULATION
MASONRY TIES

REINFORCED CONCRETE BEAM

THRU-WALL FLASHING
STEEL SHELF ANGLE
WEEP HOLES
ALUM. WINDOW FRAME

INSULATING GLASS

FLASHING
CANT STRIP
5-PLY BUILT-UP ROOFING
RIGID INSULATION
REINFORCED CONCRETE SLAB

SUPPLY AIR DUCT

FLUORESCENT LIGHT FIXTURE

SUSPENDED CEILING

triangles, compasses, and varieties of templates for drawing geo-metric shapes. As lines are drawn straighter, thinner, and more accurately, pencil leads become harder and are sharpened more frequently. Increasingly architects are drawing less and less manu-ally. Ever more sophisticated computer software and hardware make it easy to generate design drawings using computers, scan-ners, digitizers, and plotters. Computer-based design development drawings take time to construct, but once constructed, they can be studied, manipulated, plotted, and replotted as designs crystallize.

Presentation drawings can be done any time after schematic design. Unlike study sketches and carefully constructed design or working drawings, presentation drawings are explicitly made to impress clients, to show at reviews and meetings, or for publica-tion. They are documents intended to convey to nonarchitects the essential imagery of a design, to evoke positive feelings, to entice and persuade. They may be versions of drawings produced during the design development phase, rendered manually with ink, soft pencil, or other media to impart tone and texture, shade and shad-ow, and color. Often they are computer-generated drawings of multiple views plotted with a variety of line weights, colors, and textures. Whether drawn manually or by computer, they must be thoughtfully composed. Often firms make presentation drawings during subsequent phases, or even after projects are built, if they were not required prior to the construction drawings phase.

Most of the time spent producing drawings in architects' offices is consumed by the creation of detailed construction documents. Although perhaps only one or two architects generate drawings needed during the conceptual design phases, a number of architec-tural staff members may need several months to produce all of the working drawings—the detailed design—for building permits and construction. Creating construction documents is the most labor-intensive, complex, and sometimes tedious phase of the architect's work. Whether drawing manually or using CAD, as much as 50, 100, or even 150 hours can be consumed to generate and complete a single sheet of detailed construction drawings. In a full set of drawings, there easily can be ten to fifteen sheets for small projects and many dozens or hundreds of sheets for large or complex projects, not counting engineering drawings whose number can exceed the number of architectural drawings.

Turning out construction documents also entails extensive coordination within the architect's office, a process made easier with computers and database management programs. Consider the following items typical of the content of a set of architectural working drawings, applicable to either large or small projects, and necessary to describe fully the design of a building:

Drawing type	Content
Site plans	Location of buildings, other improvements, grading, paving, landscaping, utilities.
Building floor plans	Location of columns, walls, rooms, windows and doors, cabinetry, equipment, and layout dimensions.
Building sections	Profiles of building roof, floors, walls, wall openings, spaces within, ceilings, structure, and vertical dimensions.
Exterior elevations	Orthogonal views of building exterior showing geometrical shapes, materials, location of openings, doors and windows, decorative elements, assembly joints, textures and coloration (by notation).
Interior elevations	Like exterior elevations but showing the composition of interior wall surfaces, especially kitchens, bathrooms, and decorated or special spaces such as entrance lobbies or concert halls.
Reflected ceiling plans	Composition and layout of ceiling surfaces, including locations of light fixtures, ventilation registers, panels, sprinkler heads, acoustical grids, and any exposed structure, ducts, or pipe.
Schedules of materials and equipment	Tabular schedules showing the type, size, and quantity of windows and doors; interior

| | materials and finishes for walls, ceilings, and floors; painting; finish hardware (e.g., locksets and hinges for doors); light fixtures; plumbing fixtures. |
| Details | Large-scale plans, sections, or elevations of visible construction details and assembly conditions (e.g., how a window fits into a wall or a railing attaches to a floor), stairs, cabinetry and millwork, ornamentation, and other architectural components. |

Keep in mind that each single sheet of drawing may represent from one to three weeks per person of manual or computer-based design, drafting, dimensioning, and note writing. Remember too that over the lifetime of the project, several different architects may be working on the documents but not necessarily at the same time or with the same expertise.

All of these architectural drawings are complemented by analogous drawings furnished by engineers showing structural foundations and framing, mechanical equipment, ductwork, piping, electrical circuits and equipment, along with appropriate engineering details. The architects must constantly check their own work, as well as that of others, to ensure that each building component is shown and specified consistently throughout the drawings, that dimensions are consistent, that no essential item is omitted from the drawings, and that components will fit together at the construction site as they appear to fit together in the drawings. CAD software and the use by all parties of a common design database have made coordination easier and more reliable.

As you may have observed, architect's working drawings are typically covered with notes. These are an integral part of building design drawings, though in verbal form, explaining and specifying what cannot be shown graphically. They identify and name components and materials or instruct contractors to perform specific work in accordance with the notation. For example, one note might identify a material as "concrete," whereas another might say that each batch of concrete is to be tested before placement. Often notes like the latter are contained in specifications written and printed separately from the drawings.

The need to write words on drawings gave rise to the architect's art of lettering, once a time-consuming part of the work of draftspersons. Most lay-people can recognize the hand printing of an architect, perfected after hours and hours of practice and repetition, drawing lettering guidelines and struggling to make an ideally shaped "S," "B," "R," or "M." Many architects still can letter quickly and beautifully, but the need for this skill has greatly diminished, since titles and notes are now typed on the computer keyboard.

Firms have a tendency to optimize productivity by employing people who work fast and effectively in at least one area of activity. Since the greatest percentage of time and labor goes into the production of construction documents, primarily working drawings, firms prefer to hire architects who have CAD mastery and know how to perform detailed design for construction. One or two senior design partners, responsible for generating fundamental design concepts, can keep scores of junior architects busy in front of computer screens if there is enough new work coming into the office. Therefore, young architects hired by any but the smallest of architectural firms are likely to be put to work primarily on producing construction documents. Although it is essential to spend some number of years early in your career producing such documents to learn the art and craft of design for construction, it may not be your life's ambition.

Some young architects, having demonstrated exceptional design and graphic talent as students, are hired expressly to be designers. Concentrating on the schematic design and design development phases of work, they may have little opportunity to produce detailed construction drawings and specifications. The graphic ability to make beautiful presentation drawings tempts firms to keep such people doing what they do best. Other architects develop a reputation as "field" types if they prove effective in handling construction contractors and job site problems, preparing field reports, and following up at the office with memos. If so classified, such architects may rarely produce drawings.

Writing

As you can see from table 9.1, a number of functions in architectural practice entail little or no drawing. However, virtually all functions require some time invested in writing, reading, and talking— basic verbal skills that are critical to practicing architecture. To the surprise of many graduate architects newly employed in architectural offices, much time is spent writing. They write letters or memoranda to clients, engineers, product manufacturers, and government agencies. Memos and reports must be prepared, sent, and filed constantly. Architects must write specifications, some in the form of notes on drawings, transmitting information about their design intent to others. Architects with management responsibility write proposals, contracts, certifications, and promotional documents.

Specifications can be the bulkiest written output of an architectural practice. To beginning architects, a set of construction specifications can appear intimidating, not only because of its size but also because of the esoteric nature of many of the items called for. Nevertheless, most sets of specifications are merely rewrites of previously used sets, edited on the word processor to fit the project at hand.

Much of the jargon and legalese in specifications is probably unnecessary, and certainly much of it is standardized boilerplate language that could be incorporated by reference to widely accepted standards of construction practice. In fact most firms use standardized, computer-based specification formats that could be so referenced. Specifications designate materials and products to be used, identifying their type, manufacturer, size, and other performance characteristics. For example, a spec could describe the type of lumber or steel to be used in framing the structure of a building, the type of concrete for foundations, the type of windows and brick for exterior walls. Specifications are written and formatted in sections that relate to primary building trades and product categories, such as plumbing, metals, carpentry, concrete, masonry, or sitework.

For each project, the architects responsible for writing specifications must accomplish three missions: (1) delete inapplicable or obsolete specification items from the reference set; second, (2) when necessary, modify items left in to conform to the new design; and (3) add new specification items, not contained in the reference set, if the design calls for them. The greatest dilemma in preparing specifications is knowing how much to include and how much to leave out, for specifying too much or too little can get architects into trouble. Too much can drive costs up needlessly; too little can compromise quality. Only experience writing specifications and administering construction can give you the knowledge needed for resolving this eternal dilemma.

Most architectural liabilities arise only when projects are built. Therefore litigation-conscious architects tend to create and leave written paper trails comprising a history of the project: minutes of meetings, telephone notes, memos confirming verbal agreements and approvals, and letters of transmittal, among others. Thorough documenters are hard to find, since architects would rather design than write in most cases. Thus, compulsive and reasonably articulate writers are invaluable, especially during construction.

The ideal paper trail exculpates and protects the architect when things go wrong, attributing as much as possible to the contractor's mistakes or the client's poor judgment. Inspection reports, change orders, payment certifications, and general correspondence must always be written with an eye on the potential for litigation if anything done erroneously is admitted by the architect. Obviously it is in the architect's interest to cast favorable light on his or her actions and never to admit negligence. Again, like writing specifications, creating a proper paper trail is a matter of knowing what to include and what to exclude.

In many ways the most difficult and critical writing for practicing architects relates not to project documentation but rather to promotion, client contact, and public relations. Principals of firms must spend substantial amounts of time writing prose—for proposals, for portfolios and brochures showing their work, or for explaining and justifying their design philosophy. Unlike technical writing, such prose must be artful but pithy, discursive but rhetorically fine tuned. Writing text for proposals is especially important; even a simple turn of phrase can jump out, either convincing or dissuading a prospective client.

Reading

We architects read a lot. Obviously we must allot time for reading incoming mail, memos, magazines, and professional journals, like everyone else in business, whether in hard copy or on a computer monitor. We must also read and analyze research reports, reference books, manuals and handbooks, zoning and building codes, product catalogs, specifications, and contracts. And we must read them fairly carefully, with total comprehension. Failing to do so can lead to legal, financial, and professional disaster.

Not all reading is driven by legal considerations. Architects should read regularly as part of their continuing self-education. They should know what is happening in the profession, keeping abreast of new projects, new ideas, new trends, and new theories. To be informed and active citizens of their community, they should read local newspapers, not only to follow current events but also to learn about prospective project opportunities in their own community.

Talking

In this context, "talking" means engaging in substantive verbal communication of ideas or information. Just as we may be astounded by the time demands of writing, we also may be surprised by the number of hours architects devote to talking: with one another and with clients, consultants, public agency officials, committees and boards, salespeople, manufacturers' representatives, attorneys, accountants, insurance agents, and bankers. Much of this effort occurs with at least one telephone next to at least one ear. Meetings abound in architectural practice. There are days when an architect feels that architectural practice should be renamed architectural prattle.

Perhaps the most critical talking takes place when architects are selling their services, trying to develop business contacts and secure commissions, and then later when presenting and trying to sell their design concepts to skeptical clients or review boards. This kind of talking entails the art of persuasion and negotiation. The ability to convince others of your credibility, correctness, skill, and even lovability is indispensable. Indeed, the importance of public speaking skills for architects cannot be exaggerated, since architects often are called upon to stand up and talk in front of a group of strangers. Some of the world's most successful architects, despite diverse speaking styles, are masters of the rostrum. They can be at once empathetic and charismatic, articulate and expressive, perhaps even poetic. With spoken words and body language, they connect personally and persuasively with their audience, claims of discomfort or stage fright notwithstanding.

The art of speaking must be practiced when dealing with contractors, many of them tough negotiators who think nothing of having verbally reticent, taciturn architects for breakfast. Architects spend lots of time in conversation with construction estimators and project managers, superintendents, and subcontract trade foremen haggling over bids and prices, the intent and interpretation of drawings and specifications, scheduling, cost extras and overruns, and, above all, the quality and craftsmanship of construction work designed by the architect.

Calculating

"Calculate" refers to the many different types of accounting and mathematical operations that architects must perform in practice. Some accounting activity in the management of the firm's finances involves keeping track of work completed and worker hours consumed, invoicing clients and collecting fees, paying salaries and other expenses, and maintaining a sufficient supply of working capital to cover the gap between income and expenditures, since the latter often outpaces the former. This effort requires accurate, compulsive record keeping and timely (usually monthly) updating of payables (what the firm owes) and receivables (what is owed the firm).

Another kind of calculating cited in table 9.1 relates to the many quantitative aspects of project design: preliminary estimates of construction costs; construction bids; the footages and dimensions of programmed spaces and areas in buildings; zoning, site, and building code parameters (area, yard dimensions, building sizes and heights, occupancy, fire egress); quantities, sizes, and costs of components specified; building dimensions; and, in engineering design, types and magnitudes of loads imposed on engineered systems (structural loads, heating and air conditioning loads, ventilation requirements, water and sewer demand, electrical loads, excavation quantities for cut and fill, and others). Although consulting engineers may undertake the detailed computational analyses required, the architect may determine relevant loading conditions and perform preliminary calculations. In simple construction, such as individual residences, architects often do their own structural design "accounting" using reference tables and simple formulas.

Architects prepare only very rough construction cost estimates, approximations with varying degrees of reliability. During the design of large, cost-sensitive projects, they and their clients often rely on independent cost estimators. On the one hand, clients expect architects to be knowledgeable about building costs, to be able to predict with some accuracy how much any project will cost to construct (excluding the costs of land, financing, fees, and furnishings). On the other hand, most general contractors know that a project's cost can never be pinpointed accurately until the construction documents are completed, and they are usually skeptical about cost estimates done by architects.

Contractors' detailed bids are based on exact quantity surveys of construction drawings, a process in which estimators compute the quantity and cost of installing each and every item needed to construct the project as designed and shown on the drawings. Since estimates are needed before working drawings are finished, and even before design is begun, what can architects and owner/clients do? They use comparables. If a comparison can be made between the project being designed and other similar projects whose costs are known, then a somewhat realistic estimate can be generated.

To ensure comparability, the architect must consider the geographic location, size, complexity, quality, type, and time of construction of the comparable projects. Allowances must be made for inflation if data are not very recent. Most comparable cost data are expressed in dollars per square foot of enclosed building floor area, although cost figures may also be stated for other units of building size (such as volume, number of beds, or number of parking spaces). Such estimates, no matter how carefully made, are always intelligent guesses. Rarely are any two project designs or sites wholly comparable, and there are always enough special conditions to introduce large margins for error.

Architects' optimism contributes additionally to errors in preliminary estimating, as architects are notoriously consistent in underestimating the ultimate costs of their designs. This accounts in part for their reluctance to guarantee an absolute construction cost in their agreement with clients. If they did, they would often be obliged to redesign and redraw their projects, going bankrupt in the process. Prudent architects do their best to predict construction costs conservatively, hoping to look good when bids match or fall below their estimates. At the same time prudent clients should always add a healthy contingency to architects' estimates, no matter how conservative. It has been said that any good architect was not trying hard enough if the project designed was bid within budget.

Model Building

Building models is an activity familiar to all architectural students and intern architects. Few competent architects would design a project of any size or consequence without making one or more scale models, usually during the schematic and design development phases. Model making is very labor intensive, the amount of time required depending on the complexity of the design and the overall size of the model. Anyone who enjoys using his or her hands, who can derive inherent pleasure from crafting something carefully and beautifully, will probably be a good model maker. Of course, if one is overly laborious and painstaking, to the point of never finishing, then the love of craft may be superseded by the boss's concerns for time and money. No matter how fast or careful, model builders must have patience, steady eyes and hands, a concern for edges and joints, strong glue, and a sharp knife.

But architects can build another kind of model that eliminates the need for craftsmanship. Computer-based visualization programs allow us to create digital models. Building a computer model can take as much time as crafting a real, three-dimensional model, if not much more time, and it can never match the tactile,

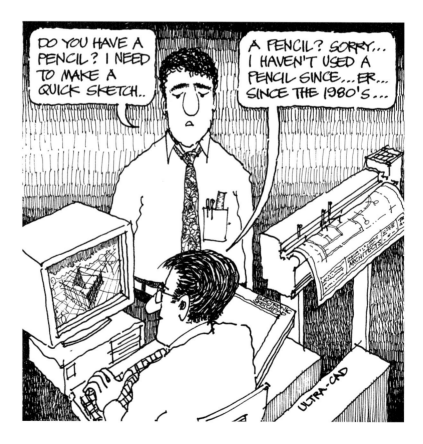

physical qualities of a model constructed of real materials. Yet computer models, once built, are extraordinarily powerful visually. First, we can represent the geometrical form of a design in a mathematically correct perspective view, and we can choose any viewpoint we want. Second, by ascribing specific attributes to each surface and solid in the digital model, we can represent almost unlimited combinations of colors, patterns, textures, and materials, including glass. Third, we can simulate diverse lighting conditions—varying sun positions and time of day and year, testing artificial lighting options—to see what the design looks like as conditions change. Lighting visualization programs also show reflections, shading, and shadows. Fourth, we can control and manipulate the model's context, its "entourage." Using photographs or other visual data, the model builder can place the project visually in its real setting, then add or subtract landscaping, people, furniture, automobiles, other buildings, or anything else in the CAD kit of parts.

Moreover, once a complete digital model of a design is built, animation programs allow us to simulate the experience of moving around, over, or through the model. We can visit the project on foot, in a wheelchair or on a bicycle, in a car or in a plane flying overhead, traveling along any path we choose at whatever speed we choose. Zooming functions allow us to move close in or far away as our perspective changes. And we can build and travel through models of not only single buildings, but also complexes of buildings, natural and constructed landscapes, towns, or cities.

There is great joy in constructing a model of a design you have created, then examining and experiencing it from a variety of perspectives. And there can be joy in building a model for a design you like, but created by someone else. However, there is little joy in making models of projects whose design you dislike or cannot respect. Unfortunately many young architects have been obliged to labor for what seems an eternity, building models of unloved buildings. This is a rut to avoid in the road to practice.

Client Contact

Client contact is among the most critical activities in architectural practice. When the design team meets periodically with the client to discuss design ideas and review progress, vital decisions about design are often made. This is when new ideas as well as conflicts may emerge, when basic formal or technical strategies are adopted, when the realities of budgets and schedules must be confronted. Indeed, the face-to-face interaction between architects and clients can disclose most clearly the differing agendas of each party, as well as offer the opportunity to reconcile those agendas.

Young architects in large firms frequently complain that they never get to meet or work directly with the firm's clients. There may be several reasons for this. First, they may be too junior in the hierarchy to attend client meetings, perhaps already overcrowded by the presence of a senior partner, a design partner, a project manager, and a job captain. Second, they may be perceived to be (how can I put it?) unpresentable. The boss may think that a particular architect-employee speaks poorly or inappropriately, dresses offensively, or otherwise poses the risk of embarrassment. He or she tolerates the employee for other purposes. Third, some clients prefer to meet only with the nominal head of the firm, notwithstanding the sometimes minimal role played by that principal in carrying out the project. Fourth, there may exist intraoffice jealousies, rivalries, and resentments between individuals. One architect may feel threatened or intimidated by another, perhaps because of differences in skills, talents, or personality.

But in almost all small and most medium-size offices, both senior and junior architects interact routinely with clients, in part because younger architects may have been assigned a greater share of project design responsibility. This is, in fact, one of the distinct advantages of working for smaller firms. No matter what their size, responsible firms ensure that intern architects have the opportunity to meet with clients, to understand the client's point of view, and to appreciate better the complex forces affecting design.

Government Approvals

Another noteworthy subroutine in the day-to-day life of the architect is the struggle with various government agencies that have jurisdiction over projects. A portion of every architect's time is devoted to persuading local building and zoning departments, zoning appeals boards, design review panels, or planning commissions that a proposed design is lawful, conforms to all of the confusing and often conflicting regulations promulgated by government agencies, and is in the public interest. To accomplish this, architects may have to meet with multiple agencies, submitting design drawings for review to each appropriate agency. There may even be public hearings requiring that the architect, along with the client and perhaps an attorney, explain and justify the project. Thus the process of obtaining government approvals can be very time-consuming.

When beginning to design a project, responsible architects search through applicable building codes and other ordinances for the requirements and standards applicable to the project. Yet that is never sufficient to ensure code compliance, which is why some architects make an effort to become acquainted with agency officials who can help unravel regulatory mysteries or resolve conflicting interpretations of poorly drafted ordinances. Unfortunately, not all officials, many of whom feel overworked and underpaid, are cooperative. Nevertheless, there are always a few officials in every jurisdiction who defy the bureaucratic stereotype, believing that their mission is to make life easier for citizens. In any case, dealing with government agencies, as with clients and contractors, demands keen negotiating skills, sensitive diplomacy, flexibility, and firmness.

Relief comes with final approvals and issuance of building permits. Conversely, the architect can learn that despite all attempts to conform to codes while conferring repeatedly with officials, the permit has been denied or delayed because of failure to comply 100 percent with regulations, or worse, criteria have changed since last checked. This bit of news may precipitate a fast trip to the permit office with pencil and paper in hand, where the architect perhaps can modify the set of permit drawings on the spot, always trying to maintain a smile. Remember that most reviewers feel obliged to find something wrong, lest their jobs or purpose be challenged.

Consultants and Coordination

Collaboration, not confrontation, is the way architects can and should work with engineering and other consultants. Ideally engineering consultants should join the project design effort not long after the architect's work has started. Once schematic design is underway or completed, engineers can study the architect's design concept and begin to formulate appropriate engineering strategies, advising the architect accordingly. As design development moves forward, preliminary engineering drawings may be started. During the construction documents phase, all of the drawings and specifications, architectural and engineering, must be prepared and, most critically, coordinated. The coordination process is crucial because the work of each participant affects the work of all the others. Normally the project architect or job captain is responsible for coordination, accomplished by periodic progress meetings and telephone conversations between architects and engineers and by transmitting computer-based data and drawings back and forth.

Despite computers, the coordination challenge can be staggering. Inside any building there are places where elements of structure (such as beams or columns), ductwork, pipes, conduits (such as electrical and telephone), and walls all want to occupy roughly the same space at the same time, an obvious impossibility. Yet each element is a necessary component of a necessary system contributing to the building as a whole, and many of these elements are shown in more than one drawing. Designs and design database drawings are built up in layers. Thus, the coordinating architect's job is to identify, visualize, and configure these elements, layer by layer, to avoid conflicts and show them consistently on each layer. If conflicts slip through, they are usually discovered when the condition is encountered by the contractor in the field. The contractor may then stop work, alert everyone, request a solution, and mentally

pocket the extra funds he is entitled to claim for the extra work caused by the coordination error. In turn, the client may claim payment from the architect or engineer.

Computers and Design

Computer technology has all but eliminated the need for conventional drafting and traditional information management techniques in architectural offices. Interlinked computer terminals and databases, with ever larger data storage devices, allow architects to keep in readily accessible digital memory: virtually all of their

business and project records, including drawings and correspondence; mailing lists, lists of consultants and contractors, and any other useful lists; frequently used or standardized documents, specifications, details, and drawings; product information, including sources; construction cost data (which must be periodically updated); and general reference data, including building codes and regulations. The Internet provides almost instant access to information, institutions, and people around the world.

Computers help us draw, visualize, process, and transmit information. CAD systems and software are especially effective, if not indispensable, in designing large, complex projects. But the computer, invaluable as it is, still is just a tool. Unable to think critically or generate ideas, it will never replace the architect. Human beings still must conduct research, visit sites, communicate with clients and colleagues, study and analyze information, coordinate the efforts of others, and, above all, engage in the always demanding and exciting act of design. Computers make it possible for us to design more effectively and more inventively. Yet with all the computer power imaginable, a mediocre architect is still likely to produce a mediocre work of architecture.

Construction Services

Construction phase services and activities contrast sharply with all previous phases. During construction of a project, architects spend most of their time doing one of four things: (1) visiting the job site periodically to make inspections or attend on-site progress meetings with the contractor, owner/client, subcontractors, engineers, inspectors, or suppliers; (2) reviewing shop drawings, usually in the office, submitted by the contractor and subcontractors; (3) clarifying or changing the design shown in the construction documents, including making final selections of colors or materials not previously specified; (4) writing reports, memoranda, certifications for payment, and letters to the owner/client, contractor, government agencies, lenders, or file.

The first activity is the most interesting. It is characterized by frequent scheduled and sometimes unscheduled trips to the site, which can be very close or very far; oceans of mud or debris at the site, necessitating ownership of at least one pair of very good, high, waterproof boots and a hard hat, which many architects keep at the ready in their car; exposure to the risks of rain, snow, ice, heat, cold, and projecting rusty nails; inevitable disputes or shouting matches between parties before, during, or after job site meetings; the thankless task of having to tell the construction superintendent that work in place will have to be torn out and redone, and at the contractor's expense; the recurring feeling of being persona non grata; and, perhaps most memorable, the elation or disappointment felt when your design, previously realized only on paper, is seen in fully constructed form for the first time.

Many architects consider the second activity, reviewing and checking shop drawings, to be one of the most boring and tedious of all the architect's jobs. A shop drawing is a detailed drawing prepared by the fabricator of a particular system or part of a building—such as steel reinforcing or structural members, cabinetry, special equipment installations, railings, curtain wall assemblies—and supposedly based on the architect's design drawings. The shop drawing, not the architect's drawing, is used to manufacture the components to be furnished and installed by the general contractor and subcontractor. Shop drawings are sent to the architect and engineers because the fabricator, subcontractor, and general contractor all want to be sure that what is made complies with the design and will fit into the building. If it does not comply, then the architect's and engineers' responsibility, after uncovering discrepancies, is to alert the contractor by disapproving the submitted shop drawing. Ordinarily this is accomplished by marking on the shop drawing (in red) and requesting a resubmittal. However, even after a shop drawing is approved, ensuring compliance with the design is still the fabricator's responsibility, not the designer's.

In large projects, there can be hundreds of shop drawings with thousands of dimensions and many opportunities for error. You can imagine what it might be like to process and scrutinize every one of these drawings. They are supposed to be submitted well in advance of the time when installation is scheduled, but sometimes they are not. Contractors often dump loads of shop drawings in the architect's lap over a short period of time, only to claim later that the completion of construction was delayed because the architect and engineers were slow or late in reviewing them. In the best of circumstances, shop drawings should be submitted many weeks ahead of installation to allow everyone enough time to correct, coordinate, fabricate, and deliver.

Completing construction of a project—bringing it to a truly final conclusion—can be a complex end game played out by the key participants. To complicate matters, there are two distinct completion points: substantial completion, when a building can be occupied but is not quite finished, and final completion, when absolutely everything is finished. Between substantial and final completion, there is a convergence of actions. First, the architect thoroughly inspects the building, inside and out, and prepares for the contractor a "punch list" of still unfinished, missing, or improperly installed items. The contractor and subcontractors, having substantially completed the project, tend to lose interest and even demobilize as they begin to focus their attention on other projects starting up or under way elsewhere. Consequently, they often drag their feet in performing the last 2 or 3 percent of the work itemized on the punch list, items that can be aesthetically crucial to the quality of the building.

Meanwhile the financial end game is playing out. The owner/client still owes the contractor money, usually including a retainage (monies earned but held back) to ensure completion. The contractor may have pending claims for extras, hoping to collect more than the original contract called for while waiting for monies already due. Each may try to play hardball, the contractor refusing to finish the work, the owner refusing to release any more funds. And there may be other pending disputes. Under standard AIA contracts, the architect, presumed to be the mediator between owner and contractor, tries to get both parties to reach agreement on what remains to be done, what is owed, and how funds finally will be disbursed. Timing is key, since the goal is to get the project from substantial to final completion on schedule. As you might guess, architects sometimes underestimate the amount of time that all of this can take. And like many other aspects of practice, finishing and closing out a project requires negotiating more than design skills.

Organization Within Architectural Firms

An architectural firm may comprise one, ten, or a hundred architects. Large firms may also include engineers, landscape architects, interior designers, computer system managers, cost estimators, and marketing and public relations specialists. Secretaries and other administrative assistants make up the support staff. But how are firms structured so that each member of the firm knows where he or she is in the hierarchy or pecking order?

Size of firm is a big factor in determining firm structure. A one-person firm is simple to organize, since one person plays all roles. When there are two or more people, however, things become much more complex, and firms with more than five or six people border on becoming institutions. Legally, most firms are either sole proprietorships, owned entirely by a single individual, or partnerships of two or more owners. There can be any number of partners. Firm owners, whether sole proprietors or partners, are entitled to the firm's profits, but they also assume responsibility for its losses and liabilities. Owners set firm policy, make final decisions, hire and fire personnel, and enjoy other benefits of business ownership.

Some states allow architectural firms to be incorporated, but the individual architects who own the firm's stock and direct its affairs are still personally liable for professional negligence in the firm's work. Incorporation offers other benefits related to deferral of income for pensions and retirement, as well as protection of personal assets from claims related to nonprofessional business liabilities. Otherwise corporations operate much like partnerships. In all forms of organization, the architects who own the firm must provide the financing necessary to start and sustain operations.

Most firms structure themselves internally in two ways: by rank or by function. Rank-structured firms are headed by one or several senior partners, typically the original founders of the firm. Below them are other partners, who may play differing functional roles within the firm. Then come senior associates, experienced staff members who help manage and may share in part of the firm's profits but who are not owners of the firm. Finally comes the professional staff, usually the youngest members of the firm. In large offices they populate the studio spaces and do most of the CAD work. Many of them may be unregistered interns, only a few years out of school. In smaller firms, such ranking is less noticed, although there are still employers and employees.

Of greater interest here is the functional structure of architectural firms, which entails two broad areas of activity: firm operations and project operations. Firm operations such as business development, marketing and public relations, personnel management, and financial management are normally supervised by senior partners assisted by appropriate staff members. These partners are primarily responsible for obtaining the firm's commissions, representing the firm to the outside world, and overseeing the general internal management of the firm.

Project operations—the set of activities that directly generates the firm's income and most of its expenses—are often characterized by a project team approach. The team may vary in size with each phase of a project, or one person may play more than one position on the team. A typical team structure consists of the following players:

Partner in charge Usually a senior partner who may have been instrumental in marketing, making contact with the client and bringing in the commission. Acting primarily as a front person, he or she may not spend much time turning out the work itself.

Project designer/architect A partner or senior associate who takes primary responsibility for the conceptual design of the project, the lead author of the work; may also be the partner in charge.

Job captain/project manager Usually an experienced associate, who may also be the primary designer, responsible for managing the day-to-day flow of work on the project, including coordination with consultants, maintenance of project records and correspondence, and supervision of production of project drawings and specifications.

Architectural designers The professional staff members who do most of the labor-intensive drawings, whether produced manually or with CAD systems, including building real or digital models; they may meet clients, hassle with contractors and building code officials, and, if talented, do schematic design and graphics work.

Secretaries/administrative assistants In some ways the most important members of any business organization of any size, they are frequently the only people in the office who know how to enter and retrieve computer-based data, how much money is in the bank, who works for the firm, where everything is located (whether in a computer file or a filing cabinet), who is supposed to meet with whom (and when and where), and what everybody earns. Like the client getters, they are truly indispensable.

Project teams also may be created through departmentalization within larger offices. Thus there may be a design group, a production (contract documents) group, a specifications group, an interiors group, a cost-estimating group, and a construction administration group. Each group or department may be headed by a partner and senior associates responsible for management of their department's activities. This means that a manager could be supervising work on several projects at once. In A/E firms the engineering departments may also be large; some have more engineers than architects and would be more correctly labeled E/A firms. Departmentalized firms may be very efficient in producing work because of specialization, but they also create artificial barriers and competition between departments. I suspect that most young architects prefer the team approach, since working on a project team in a big firm can be like working in a small firm.

Other Services

Much of this book and this chapter focuses on architecture as the design of buildings, describing the design process and how architects participate in that process. But practicing architects and firms increasingly have expanded the services they offer and the professional activities they pursue beyond designing buildings. This is not surprising given the multidisciplinary scope of architectural education in North America, the range of skills and interests many architects acquire, and the proliferation of environmental challenges posed by an ever more complex society and physical landscape. Therefore it is not unusual to find architects performing services that at first seem only marginally architectural yet clearly inhabit the realm of environmental design—for example, strategic, regional master planning, ranging in scale from counties to cities and towns; master planning and urban design for new communities, educational campuses, and other building complexes such as business parks; urban design for sectors or specific sites within existing cities, including creating new zoning regulations and design codes; and miscellaneous design consulting—advising corporations, communities and neighborhood associations, local governments, school boards, historic preservation organizations, civic and nonprofit groups. Persistent urban and suburban problems are likely to continue providing architects opportunities to confront such problems.

The Goals of Architectural Firms

To bring this chapter to a conclusion and lead you to the next, briefly consider the various goals firms pursue, either explicitly or implicitly. Explicit firm goals are rarely stated anywhere outside firm brochures, most of which promise great design done within budget, on schedule, efficiently, effectively, and for reasonable cost. The implicit goals are more telling and are evidenced by the kind and quality of work a firm does rather than by what it says it does.

With this in mind we can generally categorize goals as follows:

1. *Quality* of *design* over all else.
2. *Design innovation* over all else.
3. *Professional reputation* and *fame* over all else.
4. *Service* to the *client* over all else.
5. *Service* to the *community* and *public* over all else.
6. *Business volume* and *profit* over all else.

These goals are not mutually exclusive; a firm could pursue any or all of them. But most firms tend to develop goal structures that dominate their approach to practice and contribute to their image and reputation. Thus the newly graduated architect should be sensitive to the biases of firms where employment might be sought, since such biases can be easily transmitted.

One goal is universally shared by virtually all architects in practice: to be hired by a client for a new project. Achieving this goal is the subject of the next chapter.

10

How Architects Get Work

Several times a year I receive pamphlets from the AIA or other organizations typically entitled *Marketing Your Architectural Services*. They invite architects to attend seminars or workshops on market research, sniffing out new business, public relations, client relationships, and presentation techniques.

Until the 1970s marketing was rarely addressed or acknowledged so explicitly by the architectural profession. In fact, previous generations of professionals would argue that marketing is unprofessional—an activity for those who engage in trade, the buying and selling of products, and not for those who render professional services. Actively marketing services conjured up visions of commercial advertising, self-promotion, exaggerated claims, unfair competitive practices, and even "specials" and "discounts." Yet architects have always been naturally competitive, realizing that if they just sat back, relaxed, and waited for new clients to call, they might very well starve to death.

In today's extremely competitive climate, getting work has become so time-consuming and critical an activity in architectural practice that anyone considering a career in architecture must at least be aware of marketing goals and methods, not all of which seem like marketing. We will examine the reasons clients select architects, how they select them, and what architects do to improve their chances of being selected.

Getting the First Job

The day you look for your first job in an architectural office is your first day of marketing: you are selling yourself and the services you can provide. From your perspective, the architectural firm is your client, and the best strategy is to make an initial favorable impression. Somehow you want the firm to remember you rather than others interviewed, to like your portfolio of work more than others, to be more impressed with your personal references, to feel more comfortable and confident about you in comparison to other job applicants. You want to look good, and you want your "client" to feel certain that you can and will do the best job possible.

This certainly sounds like a sales pitch. It is! And as so often mentioned in this book, the ability to persuade other people to "buy" your talent and ideas is no less essential than the ability to generate and display your ideas. Effectively selling yourself and your services requires two complementary conditions: you must have something to sell, on the one hand, and there must be a demand, a need, a market, on the other.

For that first office job, getting hired can be tough. You believe you have something to sell—the skills acquired in school—but you quickly learn that prospective employers want both skills *and* experience. You lack the latter. How, you wonder, can you ever get that first job if only experienced architects are employable? To gain experience, you must get that first job. It can seem like a vicious circle—a catch-22 phenomenon—but eventually most people find that first job. They find a job because a firm realizes it needs new help, often immediately, and believes the applicant is ready, willing, able, and, above all, available. In fact for many young architects seeking work, the first job or two is frequently the result of being in the right place at the right time. Luck and timing are always factors in the marketing process, no matter how much talent is demonstrated.

Economic Conditions

Both individual, neophyte architects and architectural firms face the same problem in getting work, in addition to competition: the uncertainty and variability of the marketplace. Jobs with firms exist only when firms have projects to work on, and projects depend on many people and forces beyond the control of the architect. General economic conditions, worldwide and nationally, and local economic circumstances greatly affect building activity and consequently the employment of architects. When credit is available and inexpensive, prices stable, and optimism high, society builds. But when money is tight and recession occurs, building slows down. Understandably architects are bellwethers, sensing shifts in building mood early in the building process through the mood shifts of clients, contractors, lenders, and other building industry participants. When it is boom or bust for the country, it is generally boom or bust for architects.

Territory

Architects' markets are geographic and territorial. Most of us make locational decisions before any other major decisions regarding our careers, and firms must do the same, at least until they achieve regional, national, or international status. Architects must decide where to be—in what state, county, city, and neighborhood—and where to build, which is not limited to only that area immediately surrounding their offices. Selecting a market territory may be influenced by factors such as potential for population and economic growth, preferences for climate and natural environment, urban or exurban amenities, lack of competition, social or business affiliations, and family considerations. Some of these factors have to do with the market itself, whereas others reflect the personal concerns of the architect.

Market territories can be very small or virtually unlimited in size. Most architectural firms concentrate on local markets, rooting themselves in towns, counties, or cities and doing most of their projects within these local jurisdictions—their home turfs. Cities like Boston, Washington, D.C., and San Francisco are metropolitan areas comprising many jurisdictions, so architects' practices, though still considered local, may cross multiple political boundaries.

Some architectural firms, as they grow and become better known, expand their territory for building to include entire states and regions: East Coast, West Coast, Midwest, and Sunbelt are familiar regions. Some architects specialize in regional architecture, designing projects whose language of form and material derives from local building traditions while responding to local climate and ecology—New England, the American Southwest, and the Far Northwest, for example. A few architects and architectural firms attain sufficient reputations and stature to enjoy national and international market territories, totally independent of where their offices are located. Their projects may be anywhere in the country or overseas. Unaffected by local market conditions, they may not even compete for local work unless it has national or international significance.

Not all firms whose markets are geographically diverse are well known or celebrated. A number of large architectural/engineering firms do specialized projects throughout the world, often involving sophisticated technologies and equipment and requiring many employees to carry out the work over several years. Yet these firms' names are not household words, either within or outside the architectural profession. They provide services mostly to industry, domestic and foreign government agencies, and real estate developers. Much of their work, though large and complex in scope, receives relatively little media attention. But they too are not overly dependent on local markets.

Types of Markets

Architects spend a lot of time thinking about the type of market or client they want to pursue. Not only must they pick their territory, they also must decide on the kinds of projects they want to do within that territory. They may be generalist architects, going after

any and all work that comes along and in which they are interested. They may choose to specialize in certain types and sizes of projects if they have a choice, such as single residences, multifamily
housing, office buildings and other commercial structures, health
care facilities, educational buildings, or hotels. They may seek only
prestigious, often generously budgeted institutional commissions
such as museums, corporate headquarters, university buildings, or
city halls. Or they may stick to the opposite end of the cost-status
spectrum, doing only tight-budget, bread-and-butter projects such
as highway strip shopping centers, low-rent offices and warehous-
es, factory structures, and moderate-income housing. Still others
specialize in historic preservation, restoring or remodeling older
buildings for new uses, regardless of project use or type. Historic
preservation represents a growing market for architects as
America's inventory of antique and technically or functionally
obsolete buildings grows.

If given the choice, most architects would probably prefer that (1)
their market territory be national or international, as well as local,
and (2) their projects be of all types, so long as they are high budget, visible, and prestigious. Obviously this is hard to achieve. In
fact, most architects end up doing what they do for circumstantial
reasons. They locate, begin practice, and establish reputations
based partly on the kind of work that first comes in and gets built.
This early work contributes to the making of a track record and
reputation, the buildup of experience that employers and clients
look for. Once on a track, it is difficult to get off, though not impossible with some luck and much effort.

Selecting Architects for Projects

Why and how do clients select architects? The rest of this chapter
answers this question in two ways. First, we will see what clients look
for, already hinted at above. Then we will explore the specific actions
architects take to make themselves known, loved, and chosen.

Many years ago, working with students in a course on professional
practice, I wrote "An Assessment of Architectural Practice," published

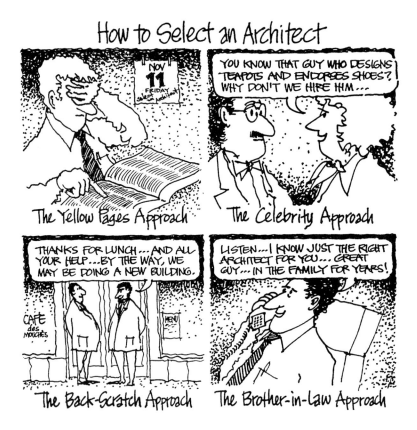

by the University of Maryland School of Architecture, in which we tried to pinpoint reasons that clients choose architects. Our conclusions were based on a limited survey in Maryland conducted by the students, who submitted questionnaires to both architects and nonarchitects. Quoting directly from the document:

Survey respondents, including architects, were asked to identify the most important considerations in choosing an architect. Following are the frequencies of response:

Design talent and creativity	50
Prior experience in similar work	33
Organization and management skills	29
Knowledge of practical aspects of building	25
Fees (cost of services)	15
Reputation	6

When asked to rank those architectural products which "sell" best, or are most in demand, architects gave highest ranking to "functional design," "competitive fees," and "economy/cost control," and lowest ranking to "building image," "aesthetics," and "innovation/novelty."

Other such surveys have been done, mostly by the AIA, and although the numbers vary, the relative distribution of responses is similar. Further, having served on several architect selection committees, I have seen evaluation forms and criteria used by public agencies to assess quantitatively and compare the qualifications of competing architects. Relative scoring weights are assigned to each of the criteria. Not surprisingly, the weighting factors are also similar to the above response distribution. Thus we can begin to understand the client's viewpoint. With no particular ranking, consider the following criteria for selection:

1. *Reputation* as to credentials and professional experience.
2. *Reputation* as to creativity, inventiveness, style.
3. *Reputation* as to personal qualities, integrity.
4. *Reputation* as to performance and meeting client goals.
5. *Reputation* as to fees, financial arrangements.
6. *Rapport* with client and others.
7. *Convenience* as to location and accessibility.

Except for items 6 and 7, these criteria are all stated as reputation: what one is known for, how one is seen by others. Use of the word intentionally suggests that a client, after selecting and working with a particular architect, may conclude that some aspects of the architect's reputation were unfounded. Nevertheless, in selecting an architect, it is the client's perception of reputation that matters, and those perceptions are shaped by the quality of evidence presented by the architect to validate the reputation.

Although most of these criteria are self-explanatory, several merit further elaboration. Take number 2, for example. Many clients are keenly interested in choosing an architect who not only is reputed to be creative and imaginative in design, but who also does work considered to be in fashion or avant-garde. They shop for specific styles by scrutinizing architectural firms' recent projects and verifying their aesthetic track records.

Item 4, performance, is critical to many clients. They look for architects who meet deadlines, whose projects are buildable within budget limitations, whose offices are neat and smoothly managed, and who can provide a long list of satisfied previous clients. This item is closely related to criteria 6 and 7 since, for all clients, good rapport with an architect is indispensable. They ask themselves: Can we communicate with each other? Does this architect understand and sympathize with our needs and problems? Are we comfortable working closely together? Do we share the same values regarding the project? Will we ever see the senior partner again?

Unfortunately, some clients associate firm size with ability to perform, assuming that only big firms can do big projects. Big firms do not necessarily perform better than small firms, although they clearly have substantial marketing and manpower advantages. Regardless of firm size, it is the project team that counts, and the team available in a small firm may be as large and capable as the team assigned by a large firm. Indeed, one advantage of small firms is that more work is likely to be done by the firm's principals and senior staff, perhaps with more commitment and care, since such projects are less common and therefore more important for smaller offices.

Matters relating to criterion 5 may be the stickiest. The architect's ideal client is one willing to pay whatever it costs to do the job right, but almost all clients are cost conscious to some degree, and for many the cost of architectural services may be a primary factor in selecting an architect. Three disparate forces act upon fee negotiations. Force one is what the client believes to be an affordable fee. Force two is what the architect believes to be an adequate fee. Force three is what the so-called market fee appears to be, that is, what the perceived competition would charge. Force one fees are generally *below* force three fees, while force two fees are generally *above*. Persuading clients to pay fair and adequate fees is not easy in this situation. Occasionally failure to agree on fees can cost architects the job, since clients always can find architects who will do the work for less money.

In addition to shopping for fee bargains, clients may also want to negotiate terms for payment of fees that are unfavorable to the architect's cash flow. Thus the total amount of the fee could pose less difficulty than how or when the fees are paid. Clients sometimes ask architects to defer receiving payment until some future date or to accept a note (IOU) or ownership interest in the project.

Nevertheless, architects who are skillful negotiators can overcome such difficulties by convincing clients that, in truth, one gets what one pays for. This requires taking time to show the client precisely what must be done to execute the project correctly, completely, and creatively. Time and cost allocations must be shown in detail so that the client understands how and why the proposed fees have been calculated. Each step in the design and construction process must be identified and explained. Once the client comprehends the scope of work and the architect's cash flow requirements, and if the client believes that the architect is the right one for the project, then architect and client usually can reach agreement, even knowing that there are other firms that would work for less.

There is a frequent exception here: governmental clients, since they may be required by statute to choose architects who, after meeting minimum qualifications, offer services for the lowest fees. For this reason many of the best architects do little or no government projects, and those who do often find that they lose money or break even doing government work. But such work can pay the rent and keep the staff busy while partners look for more stimulating and lucrative commissions.

Not all public work is frowned upon, however. Federal, state, and local governments regularly undertake prestigious projects pursued by well-known design firms. In many cases, such firms compete primarily on the basis of professional qualifications and experience, not fees. Occasionally, to select an architect for an especially high-profile project—a cultural center, city hall, airport, or public library, for example—agencies sponsor design competitions, inviting several well-qualified firms to submit preliminary design concepts which are ranked by a panel of judges. If all goes well, the top-rated competitor receives the design commission.

Sadly, a few architects, in an effort to secure commissions, have been tempted to make kickback arrangements, whereby a portion of the architect's fee, after being paid, is returned "under the table" or is "contributed" to an appropriately designated recipient. It is easy to imagine a hungry, ambitious architect agreeing to such terms with a client when the wolf is at the door and a new commission is pending. A more subtle and frequent form of kickback manifests itself when architects offer services to clients for fees that are well below cost, substantially undercutting fees prevailing in the marketplace. This is a legal but ethically questionable, and ultimately self-destructive, practice. It devalues architects' services in general, increases pressures for further fee cutting among competitors, erodes firms' profits, if any, and compels firms to continue paying relatively low salaries to their employees.

It must now be evident that architects cannot be passive practitioners in today's world. We cannot behave like sellers in a sellers' market, when in reality it is a buyer's market. We cannot assume that a combination of aptitude, talent, good credentials, and the right start will lead inevitably to success and an ample supply of work. We must go and get it, since all of our colleagues do likewise.

It also must be evident that since reputation counts for so much, getting work must mean getting *known*. Becoming and being known as an architect achieves the same purpose as it does for McDonald's or Microsoft or Mercedes-Benz: name recognition and product reputation. Architects are compelled to find ways to promote themselves, advertise their work and their ideas, and let clients and the community know who they are. As we shall see, some architects do this overtly, some in more subtle ways. Some efforts verge on commercial advertising, whereas others lead more indirectly to notoriety and favorable repute. However, any one of the activities described here can in some fashion contribute to making an architect known and in turn help to get work.

Remember too that not all architects engage in all of these activities. Indeed, some are thought to be unprofessional, or even unethical, by many architects.

The Direct Approach

The most obvious strategy for getting work is to go after projects directly, using one of several strategies.

1. Follow project leads; call on and cultivate prospective clients; read newspapers, magazines, journals, government, and business publications, looking for items that advertise or mention future or pending projects; write letters expressing interest to prospective clients.

2. Publish and distribute brochures, illustrating the firm's work, capabilities, and qualifications. Such brochures must be updated periodically and are sometimes tailored to appeal to certain types of clients. Always mention awards, special project features, and prestigious client references.

3. Issue press releases to local newspapers or national journals, announcing "news" such as awards received, new projects, or changes in address or personnel. Some firms disseminate desktop-published newsletters on a regular schedule.

4. Enter design competitions, if time and finances permit. There are always several local, regional, national, and international competitions in progress, and although the chances of winning may be remote, you can have fun doing them—and they can be added to your brochure, portfolio, or resumé.

5. If all else fails, you can advertise (once considered unethical by the AIA). Paid commercial advertising in mass media—newspapers, magazines, journals, and on radio and television—is legal, but because many architects find it unprofessional and very expensive, few engage in it; however, many firms do act as sponsors for, and contribute money to, public interest or trade organizations, which often acknowledge such gifts publicly in magazines or radio broadcasts.

The Indirect Approach

The indirect approach to promoting oneself or one's firm is more common. Rather than focusing directly on a prospective client or market, architects can enhance name recognition and reputation through activities that are noncommercial, more subtle, and perhaps more effective than the direct approach—ways that many deem to be more professional than simply asking someone to hire them.

1. Be socially active. Entertain people, especially those who might be potential clients or might refer clients to you. Memberships and active participation in appropriate clubs or social organizations may prove fruitful, expanding your network of acquaintances.

2. Join and participate in various civic, business, and professional organizations. Architects can not only make useful contributions to the community, but also meet many influential people, further expanding the network of contacts and potential clients.

3. Publish work, usually finished projects, in local, regional, or national media such as newspapers and professional journals. Home town newspaper articles can have the same effect as advertising, and exposure in professional and trade journals builds reputation among both colleagues and prospective clients.

4. Give lectures and speeches to community groups and schools, and attend conferences. Participation in seminars, workshops, and other educational programs also contributes to name recognition and reputation.

5. Submit projects to win awards in local, regional, and national awards competition programs, most of which are for design. This requires properly documenting (photos, slides, presentation drawings) and submitting work on a fairly regular basis. Expect recognition to be periodic, since work awarded depends largely on the tastes and moods of design awards juries; publicize such awards whenever possible.

6. Write about architecture, either articles or books—if you have time, since writing is very time-consuming. Any subject will do if

someone will publish it, although controversial subjects and personal manifestos may attract the most attention.

7. Get others to write about you if you have done something significant or have become sufficiently interesting. Being the subject of someone else's writing, even as the object of criticism, can establish you as a "famous" person in the eyes of the reading public and among many reading architects and architectural aficionados. This is accomplished most readily when you have friends in the media, particularly architectural journalists.

Self-promotion by architects is easiest when their work is newsworthy or when they become so well established that anything they do or advocate gains an audience. Becoming recognized, respected, and famous is difficult for those who do only competent work and almost impossible for those who do poor or uninteresting work. But it may also be difficult if they make no effort explicitly to promote themselves using the tactics outlined. It is not enough just to be good at what you do, to be an expert or a great talent. Something more is needed: you must be willing to tell the world what you can do.

Assuming that an architectural firm has established itself and enjoys some kind of positive reputation, it still must face the reality of stiff competition, since typically many firms are qualified for a given project at a given time. This means that at some point, firms must use the direct approach to obtain commissions, no matter how successful they have been utilizing the indirect approach. How, then, do clients and architects finally get together?

Generally, architects are selected to do a single project. Unlike doctors, lawyers, or accountants who usually have continuing relationships with clients over extended time periods, the architect may do only one project for a particular client. If hired again by the same client, it is on a project-by project basis. Nevertheless, many successful firms pride themselves on the amount of repeat business they get from satisfied clients who keep coming back for more.

More typically clients hire architects with whom they have not worked before. They find and select them mostly through these avenues:

- Personal contact, either social or professional
- Referral, based on reputation and experience
- A screening process, based on professional qualifications
- A screening process based on fees
- Client-sponsored design competitions

Indeed, architectural firms get much of their work through referrals and personal contacts. Even then, they must sell themselves, since clients often interview several architects before making their final choice. By contrast, government projects, once set in motion, are first announced in newspapers and other periodicals with a request for all interested design firms to submit letters of interest and statements of qualification. Agency screening committees then narrow the list of interested firms to those few they want to interview. After interviewing firms remaining on the "short list," they make their choice. Often a similar approach is taken by non-governmental institutions when selecting an architect.

The Interview

Skill is required to woo and sign a client, and it must be applied especially effectively in that most critical of architect/client encounters, the interview, of which there can be more than one to obtain a commission. An interview is like a first date; initial impressions are lasting and powerful. Interviewing is a performing art. When the appropriate moment arrives, the architect must make his or her move to enthrall and captivate. The romancing is done with both words and images, presented colorfully through the use of 35-mm slides or computer-generated images and animated video playback. Well-composed, slickly printed brochures, illustrating with photos and drawings the firm's relevant project experience, back up the architect's proposal document, which typically describes the proposed project team, including consultants,

the work plan and schedule, the project management approach, and sometimes even the designer's philosophy and design strategy. Architects often refer to this as their "dog-and-pony show."

Having captured a prospective client's attention, architects must convince the client that they alone possess the unique qualities sought and that their future working relationship will be ideal. Most important, they must demonstrate their profound understanding of the project and the client, their familiarity with the site and program, their insight into the project's special requirements, and their respect for the budget and schedule. Fees for services may be the last point of discussion during an interview, and these may be explored in detail only after the architect has been tentatively chosen.

Joint Ventures

To compete more effectively, architectural firms sometimes form joint ventures with other architectural firms or with engineering firms. A joint venture is a temporary partnership between two or more firms created for the sole purpose of carrying out a specific project; otherwise, the firms continue to conduct business as separate entities. Joint venturing can expand geographic coverage and broaden expertise, or it can provide a firm access to a market in which it has not been able to operate previously. Joint ventures are marriages of convenience, transforming small firms into big firms and big firms into bigger firms. Boston firms can become Chicago firms, or office-building firms can become hospital firms. Occasionally joint ventures result when clients want a "design-oriented" firm to team up with a "nuts-and-bolts" firm. In this instance, the former normally takes responsibility for the schematic and design development phases of architectural services, while the latter prepares construction documents and oversees construction.

Architects as Contractors, Construction Managers, and Developers

Some architects keep busy by offering clients construction management or "design-build" services. In the design-build mode, architects wear two hats: they act as both designers and construction managers, performing the functions normally performed by general contractors. Many design-build architects undertake only modestly sized projects, primarily residential and small-scale commercial projects such as office buildings or retail stores. But a number of diversified A/E firms have their own CM departments and provide construction management services for larger projects, directly competing with general contractors and firms specializing in construction management.

Merging architectural and contracting functions seems appealing for both architects and clients, since it reduces the number of organizations a project owner has to deal with and gives the architect full control over construction. But there are financial risks for both client and architect if the architect's cost estimates and bids are too low, or if the project is undercapitalized and monies run out before completion. A potential conflict of interest exists for the architect; although the client seeks the most and the best (within the budget) from the architect and contractor, the contractor's objective is usually to build the architect's design at the least possible cost, an incentive to cut corners and compromise quality. If the architect plays both roles, there is no mediator between the owner/client's interest and the contractor's interests. Ultimately the outcome of design-build relationships depends on the integrity and financial acumen of the architect.

A few architects act as real estate developers, designing projects in which they have a significant ownership interest. Being one's own client can be very appealing. The architect-as-developer strategy represents a potentially rewarding but risky means for getting work. Not only can practicing architects earn substantial profits as developers, and potentially more than they can as architects, they also can exercise greater control over the final design within the limits of budgets and marketability, since they own the project. Of course, they can lose money, and lots of it, if a project goes sour. Architect-developers mostly undertake housing or small commercial projects. Often joined by other investment partners, entrepreneurial architects perform all the functions of the real estate developer—land acquisition, equity and debt financing, construction, and marketing—in addition to the design functions of the architect.

Projects developed by architects are no more likely to succeed than to fail economically. However, relatively few actively practicing architects have been both successful developers and successful architects. Many architect-developers have learned the hard way that developing projects is not at all the same as designing projects. Each requires altogether different expertise, psychic energy, business skills and attitudes. Each entails very different risks and requires different kinds of stomach linings. Nevertheless, architects always will be tempted by the perceived liberty and potential profitability of designing projects for themselves.

Design Competitions

Competing for architectural prizes or commissions on the basis of proposed designs has a long history. Many notable monuments and public buildings, and a fair number of private ones, have been built as the result of design competitions. There are several ways to conduct a design competition, but most competitions fall into one of two categories: open or invited. In an open competition, as the name implies, the sponsor generally accepts design submissions from anyone qualified to enter, although qualifications can be restrictive—for example, competitors might be limited by nationality or geographic location. In an invited competition, the sponsor, after first screening the qualifications of those architects expressing interest, selects only a few from whom design proposals are solicited. In both cases, a jury composed of professional designers and client representatives, designated by the competition sponsor, usually reviews the design concepts, ranks them, and selects the winning proposal.

Competitions can be conducted in one or two stages. In the latter instance, there are two rounds of design: a first round to narrow the field and a second round to pick the winner. In open competitions, competing designers receive no compensation for their work. In fact normally they must pay a fee to enter. In two-stage, open competitions, only the finalists who make it past stage one receive a stipend, and even then the modest fee rarely covers the costs of producing the stage-two design submission, much less the work done for stage one. By contrast, architects invited to participate in a competition among a small number of firms, whether in one or two stages, typically are paid a preliminary design fee by the sponsor. However, these fees also are likely to be nominal, well below the cost or value of the work that the firms do.

Some architects believe that design competitions are one of the fairest methods for selecting architects. Other architects hold the opposite view. The former believe that open competitions offer small firms, or relatively undiscovered architects, the opportunity to "score" quickly and emphatically, to make their mark and gain recognition against overwhelming odds, and to win monetary prizes and significant design commissions. They further argue that design competitions bring out the best designers and stimulate the most creative, innovative design thinking, bringing forth design proposals that the average or nonchalant architect, working with a conservative client, might never dream of.

Competition cynics or opponents claim that competitions are inherently unfair because the outcomes often reflect the biases of the jury that selects the winners, while failing to address and grapple with the needs or tastes of the client and project users. They claim that competitions favor either well-established architectural firms with ample financial and staff resources, allowing such firms a potential edge in presentation, or, conversely, firms whose work load is slack. Architects who are busy may have difficulty finding time to undertake competitions without compromising both the competition effort and their efforts on behalf of their regular, fee-paying clients. Another objection is that many competitions are exploitative and poorly managed, with ambiguous rules and requirements. Architects also have accused some sponsors of being exploitative, taking advantage of architects' willingness to go for the brass ring and using the competition process to obtain design ideas at minimal cost.

A very small percentage of all projects designed by architects are the result of open or invited design competitions. Frequently, winning designs are never executed because the projects are abandoned, were never real, or proved too expensive or impractical. When both a prize and a commission are awarded, the winning architect may still suffer financial loss or be decommissioned, subsequently excused from completing the work for technical, economic, or political reasons, only to have his or her design altered and executed by someone else. And in many competitions, vital interaction between architect and client during the formative phases of design is missing.

Ultimately design competitions, as a method for getting work, are a long shot for almost all architects in practice. Competition sponsors and the projects they build clearly benefit from the profusion

of ideas and the investment of thousands of hours by all the losing competition entrants. But competitors, after a costly search for success and recognition, may end up with little more than feelings of frustration, envy, and sour grapes, no matter how much fun was had participating. Yet, to be a winner . . . !

Free Services

One questionable marketing tactic is worth noting: doing work for free. For many years the AIA and the profession in general condemned the practice of furnishing prospective clients with free

sketches, designs, or other services without fair compensation. To do so was considered unprofessional and unfair. Yet this occurs frequently. It is the architect's loss leader, the come-on to attract the client's business. But there is nothing illegal about providing free services (unethical, perhaps, but not illegal).

Increased competition among architects, along with more aggressive marketing practices, puts pressure on architects to do a bit of up-front work for free as an inducement to prospective clients. This pressure is hard to resist if you believe that everyone else is doing likewise. I have participated in architect selection committee interviews during which firms, not yet selected and with no compensation, have presented unsolicited, detailed site and program analyses, plus schematic design concepts, which cost many thousands of dollars to generate. This work is an integral part of basic design services and thus has measurable economic value and should be paid for. But to gain a competitive edge in pursuing commissions, many firms are willing to gamble. Sometimes it pays off, sometimes not.

You surely will face the same pressures. How much free work should you do for a prospective client, in the interest of courting that client, before you are selected and given a contract? When the contract beckons and the project promises new design opportunities, it is hard to know where to draw the line.

Let me conclude with a few general observations:

- Getting work represents a large part of the practicing architect's efforts.
- Getting work is costly.
- The chances of being hired for a project are small in the face of stiff competition and a limited supply of projects.
- Architects' marketing techniques have become more commercial in nature, with the practice of architecture transformed increasingly into the business of architecture.

Many architects voice regret over the transformation of architectural practice, but they may be voices in the wilderness. More and more promotional efforts are launched each year as the pressures of consumerism and fast fashion intensify, and as architects proliferate while projects and clients may not.

11

Architects' Clients

Most architects are employed by clients who are contemplating building something. Some architects think of clients only as sources of work and income, but most good architecture is in fact the result of a successful design collaboration between an enlightened architect and an enlightened client.

A client may be a person, a couple (married or otherwise), or an organization. Legally constituted partnerships, corporations, non-profit associations, and governments can be clients. A lawyer would tell you that an entity needs two things to be a legitimate client: lawful existence as an entity with authority to enter into enforceable contracts, and money. For architects the latter criterion may pose more problems than the former, since there are loads of clients with no funds, many clients with inadequate funds, some clients with barely enough funds, and almost no clients with unlimited funds.

Architects have great clients and difficult clients. Great clients are perceived to be sympathetic to most, if not all, of the architect's design ideas, to give the architect wide design latitude, and to spend money in the interest of creating a work of art. They are decisive yet accommodating, and they never make changes to designs once approved. Such clients also willingly pay the architect's fees and continually praise the architect's work.

Difficult clients obviously display the opposite characteristics. They question not only the architect's ideas but also his or her comprehension of their true programmatic, financial, and scheduling problems. They nit-pick, complain about costs, and make decisions slowly. Agonizing forever over each design issue, they often insist that the architect generate limitless design alternatives before agreeing to one. Even then, such clients think nothing of making further changes without consulting the architect, or they disregard entirely the architect's opinion. And of course many squawk when they receive the architect's bill, wondering how a few sheets of drawings could cost so many thousands of dollars.

Great clients respect the architect as a professional, an artist, a problem solver, and they can accept inevitable minor imperfections as part of the price of attaining lofty aesthetic goals. Difficult clients may think of the architect as a necessary but obstructive provider of costly services, insensitive to practical or economic issues, careless, egotistical, and periodically incompetent. Because many clients have only one direct professional encounter with an architect during their lifetime, that unique experience may forever color their perception of what architects are like, making them either skeptical of or believers in the value of architects and architecture.

The Household Client

Let us look at the most plentiful type of client, clients who demographically are households and who want to improve the quality of their personal living environments, their homes. Household clients, whether singles, couples, families, or communes, hire architects because they want a new residence—house or apartment—or want to remodel an existing home. In all cases, they seek more or better space, privacy, security, convenience and comfort, and, in many cases, ego satisfaction. The architect is expected to provide a design that can be built by a contractor within the client's budget and yields a functional, structurally sound, dry, easily maintained environment that is neither too hot nor too cold. But the architect and client may strive for more: they may aspire to creating a work of art.

The household client often asks the architect to design not only the building but also the interior environment: furniture, floor cover-

ings, wall and ceiling finishes, decorative trim, colors and fabrics, lighting, window treatments (drapes, shades, blinds), potted plants, artwork, and even ashtrays. The line between architecture and interior decoration can blur in household design work, since domestic interiors are the province of another profession, interior designers and decorators.

Intervention by the client, or by decorators, in designing interiors is seen by many architects as unwanted intervention. But all decorators, and many clients, hold the opposite view, insisting that architecture is concerned mostly with the exterior of buildings and, at best, only the layout and shaping of interior spaces. Inside, the will of the decorator and client, not of the architect, prevails. As a result, many well-conceived works of architecture have been spoiled by bad decorating decisions. Conversely good interior design can help cover up bad architecture.

Household clients can be the most demanding of all clients. Their project may be among the most important single undertaking of their adult lives, financially and psychologically, whether a back porch addition or a new multimillion-dollar home. Residences are personal and intimate places where ego investment is high. Unique behavior occurs there. In our homes we sleep, eat, practice hygiene, make love, read, work, recreate, communicate, socialize, or simply survey that tiny part of the world over which we have dominion.

Home represents an investment not only of money but also of self. Thus for the household client, life's most fundamental needs, desires, activities, experiences, and resources are involved. This is why people are willing to commit so much of their income (from a third to nearly half) and energy to their personal dwelling environment. It is therefore not surprising that household clients can be intensely involved, demanding, and emotionally exposed when their home is at stake.

Many clients want fur but can afford fabric. Wanting gourmet quality, they can pay only for takeout. They also expect flawless judgment from the architect, along with speedy service, ability to predict the future, and error-free design and construction. Some clients assume that architects have unlimited control of contractors and unlimited knowledge of building products, not to mention the power to ensure that construction is finished on time and without cost overruns.

For their part, architects often expect household clients to be receptive to their every design whim and proposal, to tolerate delays and errors patiently, and to be willing to increase their construction budget in the event bids are too high. Architects can fail to warn clients adequately about the limits of the art and science of architecture and construction. The imperfections and unforeseens that may in fact be acceptable to the owners of airports, office buildings, shopping centers, or schools are frequently unacceptable to home owners.

There is much more than a business relationship established between architects and household clients. To some extent, the designer must psychoanalyze the client, becoming familiar with the client's personal habits, tastes, behavior, compulsions, and feelings. The designer may even become enmeshed in the client's domestic affairs, since creating a new home can bring out repressed or unrecognized conflicts and animosities that otherwise might not be revealed. Countless architects have witnessed hostile exchanges between a husband and wife over some design issue, whereupon the architect is suddenly thrust into the role of family counselor and peacemaker. Usually the architect can mediate successfully, but sometimes building a dream house can undo a marriage.

Architects design houses mostly for fun, not for profit, although they can make a perfectly good living designing homes. Some architects are happy just to break even when working for household clients, the majority of whom cannot afford to pay the fees required to cover all the time and overhead costs. Most large architectural firms do houses only as a favor to someone. Yet house design continues to receive substantial attention in the media and from many architects, because designing houses for household clients often gives architects the best opportunity for design experimentation and formal invention. As loss leaders, residential projects also may bring bigger, more profitable work in the future, thanks to appreciative household clients of the past.

Developers

Architects would like to believe that their goals are the same as their clients' goals; they frequently are not. In particular, the architect's desire for aesthetic self-expression may be of little or no concern to the client. This is often true in the realm of commercial building, the world of profit-motivated real estate development. Commercial clients' motives are quite different from those of clients' building homes for themselves. The market-oriented client is usually interested in only one thing: economic success, measured by profit.

The majority of investment in building construction in the United States is commercial development undertaken by private business entities. It includes office buildings, multifamily housing, subdivision housing, retail shopping facilities, industrial and warehouse buildings, and recreational and entertainment facilities. Clients developing commercial properties view their projects not as artful works of architecture but rather as investments that produce income, money machines that yield a return on capital. Without the prospect of profit, such projects would never be built.

A client developing commercial property naturally tends to look for architects who design buildings that cost the least to construct and operate while simultaneously producing the greatest possible revenue. Here occurs the potential conflict between architect and client. Often the architect proposes designs that achieve the opposite, costing more to construct and operate without corresponding increase in potential revenue and hence less potential investment profit. If construction and operating costs are too high and revenues too low, the owner will lose money.

Even developers experience self-conflict in dealing with their own self-imposed economic constraints. They must select the level of design quality and amenity necessary to capture the targeted market or to generate anticipated revenues. Otherwise they risk offering too little for the price and losing the market to competitors who seem to offer more. Accordingly, the architect tries to sell good design to developer clients on the basis of sound business and investment thinking, arguing that better-quality design and increased spending will result in faster and higher rentals or sales. This is a language that commercial clients can understand, although they must be convinced.

To developer clients, the ideal architect would thoroughly understand their goals and limitations, along with building economics, would always meet budgets and deadlines, would easily obtain approvals from building officials and government review agencies, would turn out error-free, easy-to-read drawings for easy-to-build buildings, and would design buildings that work well and look good at the same time.

There is no shortage of architectural firms claiming to offer all of these things, and certainly some can deliver. Developers learn quickly about architects and the kinds of services they provide. When they find an architect responsive to their aspirations and requirements, that is the architect they will choose and stick with. As long as this mutually satisfactory relationship exists, that architect will have a loyal client. But let something go wrong, and the client will look elsewhere. Naturally there are many architects who are excellent designers but whom developers would be reluctant to hire.

To many architects the behavior, objectives, and values of commercial real estate developers seem crass and shortsighted. Architects argue that too many developers sacrifice human, cultural, or environmental ideals to the so-called bottom line, rejecting attempts by architects to design artfully. Developers, say many architects, fail to provide enough time and money to execute projects properly. They feel that some developers are abusive, demanding acquiescence, get-it-done-yesterday performance, and flawless work, all for discounted fees. Architects protest that developer clients commonly exploit architects economically, insisting that compensation for services be deferred as a condition for getting the design contract. In effect, by extending credit to the client for many thousands or tens of thousands of dollars, architects become bankers.

Some developers and architects believe that art and commerce can be successfully reconciled, although not always easily. It is more difficult to create award-winning architecture in the face of severe economic constraints than when such constraints are relaxed. Although the landscape is littered with thousands of bottom-line buildings that barely qualify as architecture, there are nevertheless many structures that have succeeded both commercially and aesthetically. Regrettably there are also a few that succeeded as architecture but not as investments.

Architects themselves have sacrificed ideals by sometimes doing mediocre work or by abandoning the commercial sector of the design market to lesser talent. Many developers support this contention by pointing to deficiencies they attribute regularly to architects: delays, cost overruns, inefficient or unbuildable designs, unworkable construction details, wasted space in buildings, confusing or incomplete drawings and specifications, incorrect use of materials, poorly coordinated structural or mechanical systems. Although developers are normally more sophisticated about construction, their expectations concerning professional performance can equal those of household clients.

An astute developer client would probably assert that creating buildings is a business, not an art, and that their tactics are just sound economic practice. If architects can participate in this business and create art at the same time, that is fine, so long as their priorities do not supersede the client's. Some architects are willing to work on these terms; others are not. With each client and project, architects must examine the prospective client's values and compare them with their own. The architect looking primarily for aesthetic patronage will usually not find happiness on the bottom line.

The Corporate Developer

The corporate developer is not just a developer whose business is legally incorporated. Rather, it is a developer operating like a corporation. Corporations of this sort are departmentalized institutions with decision-making responsibility both concentrated at the top and dispersed in the middle. They have several levels of management under the direction of officers, who answer to directors, who answer to stockholders. Specialization abounds: marketing, finance, production, construction, estimating, purchasing, accounting, project management, property acquisition, and maintenance, to name a few. Each person in the corporation has an interest in what the architect does, but colored by his or her respective area of responsibility.

When the architect designs for a corporate developer, there are really dozens of clients. Marketing managers, concerned with selling or leasing, see the design as a product to be marketed. Construction managers see it as an assemblage of materials and labor. Finance managers and accountants see projects as capital investments, cash flow projections, statements of profit and loss. Property managers see buildings as machines to be maintained after others have built and marketed them. Then there are those overseeing all: the corporation's chief executive officers and active directors. Their interests are earnings, payable dividends, increased stock value, and corporate image.

Corporate kingdoms may contain multiple territories jealously guarded by their respective territorial overlords, some of whom are subject to delusions of grandeur. Such executives are often both assertive and insecure. They want to succeed in corporate life, to aggrandize their authority and status, to perform well, if not better than their in-house competitors. Corporate managers want to look good within the company along with doing their job properly for the benefit of the company's customers and stockholders.

Architects have to cope with numerous company executives and company politics when working for corporate clients, deciphering the power structure to figure out who makes the ultimate decisions. Once understood, dealing with corporations can become a game the architect can play and, with luck, master by letting each individual in the corporate hierarchy believe that his or her opinion is indispensable, that his or her needs are paramount, while still seeking the trust and consent of the top brass.

Many corporate clients are methodical and unemotional in pursuing their goals, operating in a more orderly, well-documented fashion than other types of clients. They tend to honor contractual arrangements more readily, including payment of architects' invoices, partly because institutional rather than personal funds are involved. But corporations may also prefer to do business with other corporations. Therefore architectural firms with corporate qualities appeal to corporate clients, as if corporations had lives and egos of their own, wishing to engage in intimate corporate relations with other corporate entities.

Entrepreneurs

The most frequently encountered commercial client is the individual entrepreneur—the developer whose team is small and who may be building only one or two projects at any given time. He or she may operate using a corporate form of organization or a limited partnership, but the mode of operation clearly bears the stamp of one person and one will, unlike most corporate clients.

Entrepreneur clients come closest to being the architect's counterpart. Their egos are at stake, as well as their fortune (if they have one). They are usually willful, decisive, and outgoing, investing much of themselves in their real estate ventures. They exhibit a certain toughness and resilience, plus the ability to make decisions based on gut instinct rather than intellectual analysis. Some have a sense of mission as well as a desire for wealth. To others development is nothing more than a business in which sizable fortunes can be made or lost through financial leverage, the investment of small amounts of the entrepreneur's money—equity funds—and large amounts of other people's money—debt capital.

Historically the entrepreneurs of civilization—political, military, artistic, scientific, and religious figures—sponsored the building of great monuments or cities. The spirit, power, and will of such individual figures resulted in work for architects and builders who would have had little to do without the impetus provided by kings, queens, emperors, moguls, popes, generals, and statesmen of the past. Although the primary goals of these historic entrepreneurs were not related to financial investment opportunities, I am sure their instincts and compulsions were similar to those of today's entrepreneurial developers.

The Institutional Client

The term "institutional" can mean many things to many people and to different architects. In architectural practice, it usually refers to clients and projects other than those that are primarily investment and profit oriented, although institutional buildings often are used for fund-raising functions. Thus this definition excludes commercial real estate development whose principal purpose is to produce investment income from rents or sales. Further, institutional clients are generally organizations, corporate or otherwise, that develop projects for very specific purposes. Typical projects include:

• Civic buildings such as cultural centers, museums, performing arts facilities.

• Schools—primary and secondary schools, special schools, university buildings.

• Religious facilities.

• Health care facilities—hospitals, nursing homes, clinics.

• Institutional headquarters and administrative facilities.

• Recreational facilities such as arenas and stadiums.

Although a few of these projects may be built for profit-making reasons (such as hospitals and sports stadiums), they are not considered conventional investment real estate.

Institutional clients are much like corporate developers in their organizational characteristics, not surprising for institutions, which may in fact be legally constituted corporations. The institution itself may comprise a very large constituency, but like corporations with countless stockholders, the institution's behavior is really fashioned by a relatively small number of people who are responsible for making policy and managing the institution's daily affairs.

The architect typically works with a building committee of some sort, delegated by institutional officers, directors, or trustees, some of whom may also be members of the building committee. Others, either from within the institution or from outside, may also serve on the committee. Outside guests may be invited to participate because of their financial resources. Active or potential institutional contributors are obvious favorites for such memberships. In addition, project users may be represented on the committee.

Building committees may have substantial decision-making authority, or they may serve in a primarily advisory capacity to another final decision maker (a chief executive officer, or a board of trustees or director). In some cases, architects may have to deal with a building committee supplemented by other ad hoc, specialized subcommittees that focus on only specific programmatic and design issues. In these circumstances, architects must navigate more carefully, since multiple committees can easily be in dispute with one another. Good communication and documentation become essential, not to mention wise diplomacy.

Institutional clients may be very sophisticated, but many have little experience in dealing with architectural design and construction. In this regard, they can resemble household clients, requiring the architect to guide the process more actively. When projects are complex, institutional clients frequently hire development advisers and construction management consultants. They represent the owner's interest in dealing with architects, engineers, general contractors, subcontractors, financial institutions, and government agencies. They assist in project scheduling, administration, budgeting, cost estimating, accounting, purchasing, and contract negotiation, acting as a go-between and surrogate client. They can greatly facilitate the process of building when relatively naive institutional clients are involved, but they can also impede it if they duplicate tasks normally carried out by competent architects and contractors.

Some institutional projects have stringent budgets, whereas others may be generously funded. Some are financed privately, through fund-raising campaigns and membership dues, and some receive direct public support and governmental allocations for construction. There are many institutional projects, such as cultural facilities or corporate headquarters, where image is important. Here the institutional client must usually provide a budget adequate for such image making by the architect. For high-budget, high-prestige projects—museums, institutional headquarters, civic buildings—institutional clients tend to select prestigious architectural firms with reputations for creating compelling architectural imagery.

Architects like to do projects for institutional clients because in their view there is a much greater chance for producing memorable, newsworthy, photogenic architecture. Moreover, the number of people participating in the development of such projects inevitably increases the architect's contacts and professional exposure. And the experience of doing special projects may well lead to new project commissions of even greater prestige and expressive potential.

As to fees, institutional clients are more likely than some other kinds of clients to pay their bills, although not necessarily on time. Architects might also complain about the complexities of coping with a client who acts like a giant committee, who makes decisions slowly and quasi-democratically, and who can be at odds with itself. Design can take longer because the architect must satisfy every single person representing the institution's interest. This is even more difficult when personal interests, tastes, and ideologies creep into deliberations. In these circumstances, persuasive charisma and charm, along with persistence and patience, continue to be valuable assets.

The Government Client

Government clients are a subset of institutional clients, but government agencies and officials have sufficiently unique characteristics to merit special consideration. Architects interact with three levels of government: local (municipal or county), state, and federal. Each is composed of executive, legislative, and judicial branches. However, most projects are undertaken by specific executive agencies of government charged with specific missions. Therefore, we need to understand how government agencies behave.

Government agencies at all levels build transportation facilities, public works projects, park and recreation facilities, administrative offices, courthouses, law enforcement facilities, fire stations, public hospitals, and housing for low- and moderate-income families. Public educational facilities are built by local city or county school boards with funding help from state and federal education agencies. Unique to the federal government are projects for the military, both domestic and overseas, and embassies in foreign countries.

Governments are organized into agencies concerned specifically with these areas. Thus, we have departments of public works, transportation, housing and community development, education, parks and recreation, public safety, health, general (administrative) services, and, at the federal level, defense and state. Although funding for construction originates with the legislative budgeting process and is officially carried out under the leadership of the executive, individual agencies really provide the impetus and management for conceptualizing and implementing most projects. And, of course, agencies are themselves corporate-like bodies populated by individual human beings.

Remember that government's objectives are more complicated than industry's. Private enterprise's goal is straightforward and simple: profit. The method for achieving the goal is easily summarized: produce and sell a product. Government, however, must protect and further public health, safety, and welfare. It must promote commerce and trade, tax its citizens, provide security, deliver services, and undertake any other essential tasks that private enterprise cannot or elects not to do. Clearly this is a far more complicated mission to accomplish; although the ends may seem apparent and indisputable, the means are not.

Looking at the government agency as a client, the architect will see a collection of people, laws, and regulations whose purpose is the achievement of public objectives. Moreover, such objectives usually must be achieved at minimum cost to the taxpayer. Thus, most projects built by government are not supposed to be luxurious, flamboyant, or precedent setting. Although there are a few notable and monumental exceptions, most government agencies seek functional, efficient, conservative, proven design whenever they undertake construction.

The advantages of working for a governmental client are much like those of other institutional and corporate developer clients. First, projects may be large in scope and on occasion of monumental proportions. Large or small, they can have interesting, challenging programs and occasionally pose provocative design opportunities. Second, government-sponsored projects ordinarily serve some public purpose, and designing projects benefiting the public may in itself be a source of satisfaction for the architect. Third, the successful completion of one government commission may well lead to another in the same area of specialization. Fourth, once a contract for services is negotiated and signed, architects know that government agencies reliably pay fees earned for services rendered, unless there are disputes.

On the opposite side of the ledger reside some serious disadvantages. They are in effect a mirror image of the advantages. Projects can be banal, mundane, and architecturally unpromising, no matter how talented the architect or well intentioned the government sponsor. Fees can be ridiculously tight or inadequate, sometimes even limited by statute despite the amount of work required of the architect. Negotiating acceptable contracts with government agencies can be excruciating, particularly when officials can always argue that some firm is willing to do the project for a lower fee. And if a dispute arises later, many government agencies think nothing of holding the architect's feet to the fire by withholding fee payment, knowing that the architect has little recourse.

Perhaps the worst attribute associated with some government clients is the so-called bureaucratic mentality. Not all government officials have it. In fact, it is a characteristic not limited to government agencies. Such minds can be found in private corporations, institutions, and architects' offices. But the word "bureaucrat" has become most closely associated with government. What characterizes bureaucrats, negatively speaking? Above all, it is attitude, not competence or expertise, although these too may be in question at times. This attitude manifests itself as a can't-do, no-way approach.

The negative bureaucrat, in contrast to the positive bureaucrat, looks for reasons *not* to do or approve things. He or she plays by the book as literally as possible and, when in doubt, says no. Clinging tenaciously to rules and regulations, such persons tend to be dogmatic and inflexible. They abhor uncertainty, the realm in which architects often must dwell. They shun taking risks and responsibility for any actions that are not clearly prescribed for them in writing. Since no code or regulation can ever anticipate every eventuality, negative bureaucrats can be major obstacles in the path of creative architects.

Equally regrettable are bureaucrats who almost instinctively resist innovation, change, or experimentation, despite the potential for fruitful improvement or discovery. Many are motivated by basic job security concerns. They fear criticism and will do almost anything to cover their respective posteriors. Even more discouraging, and infuriating as well, are bureaucrats who exhibit suspicion and skepticism concerning the motives of people with whom their agency interacts. Acting ostensibly to protect the public interest and save taxpayers' money, such officials often assume that private interests are up to something: cutting corners, charging exorbitant fees, padding expenses, conspiring with other consultants or contractors. Also, like some other types of clients, they may expect an unattainable level of perfection.

Agencies themselves, being bureaucracies, can behave this way collectively. Sometimes the architect finds that negativism is the dominant policy, particularly regarding creative architectural design. For example, many school boards and departments of education have adopted regulations and specifications that permit only the most conventional of design solutions for school buildings. The U.S. Army Corps of Engineers is notorious for its strictly "engineering" approach to building design, an approach it demands from the architects it hires. Federal, state, and local housing authorities promulgate design standards and other regulations that can make it difficult for architects to develop innovative housing projects, even to save money.

Architects experience frustration in still other ways when working for governments. Changes in personnel can deter the progress of a project's design, since new contracting officials may have quite different views or interpretations of mandates from their predecessors. This can occur most dramatically with changes of administration following elections. Sometimes the project itself may be suspended or terminated. Budgets and building requirements may be altered suddenly, compelling the architect to modify or recommence the design.

Once designed, most projects built by government agencies are competitively bid, since this theoretically ensures that taxpayers will obtain the best price possible in the construction marketplace. It also means that neither the agency nor the architect knows what the project will actually cost until most of the architectural work is completed. If the budget and interim estimates have been unrealistically low, bids can come as a great shock. In some cases government agencies demand revisions by the architect, without additional compensation, or abandon the architect's plans altogether. At best, this is an embarrassment to the architect and, despite losing money, may make collecting still-unpaid fees difficult. Unfortunately this can occur with nongovernmental clients as well.

Many architectural firms never do government projects, whereas others specialize in them. Some firms thrive on collaborating with government agencies, but some, after trying once or twice, have given up, claiming they only lost money and acquired ulcers. In all cases the type of client you will have depends on the type of architect you become.

Citizens and the Community as Clients

We architects tend to be idealists and reformers, our sights set not only on aesthetic change but also on social change. Consequently some of us carry that idealism into the neighborhoods, home towns, and cities where we live and practice. Many civic-minded architects routinely offer their services—sometimes pro bono, sometimes for nominal fees—to local citizen groups and community associations in an effort to make a difference both socially and aesthetically. Community-based design centers, staffed by volunteer architects and architectural students, have been established in many jurisdictions to help tenants and home owners improve their dwellings and their neighborhoods. Practicing architects have contributed time and expertise to public schools, homeless shelters, clinics, and other organizations that lack the financial resources to hire and fully pay an architectural firm.

Architects frequently are asked to serve on neighborhood committees, municipal advisory bodies, or planning and zoning commissions. They may get paid little or nothing for their efforts, but local citizens are invariably grateful for the advice and guidance they receive. There are lots of opportunities in most communities for architects to engage directly in public service, and those who invest the time willingly and effectively are likely to be asked to do more. The challenge is knowing when to say yes and when to say no, given competing time demands. In any case, having the community as a client can be rewarding in two ways. First, it can provide that special satisfaction that comes from doing good deeds. Second, and not incidentally, it can increase your public visibility, which may lead you to other kinds of clients, some of whom you will still need.

Many architects realize that public policy directly affects the quality of the built environment as well as America's natural resources.

They also realize that government legislation directly affects the practice of architecture. Thus a very small number of architects have run successfully for public office, becoming elected municipal, county, or state officials in an effort to influence public policy. Perhaps as architects better understand and appreciate the consequences of public decision making, more of them will seek public office as a way to effectuate positive change, both for the community as a whole and for the good of architects and architecture.

12

We Who Are Architects

Arriving at this final chapter, you should have a better understanding of the profession of architecture than you did eleven
chapters ago. Of course, no book can fully convey the architectural
profession's nuances and peculiarities, its continually shifting values and methods, its daunting challenges and shortcomings. Nor
can a book fully portray the remarkable diversity of individuals
who call themselves architects. Nevertheless a few additional
pages may help round out the book's portrait of architects and the
culture in which they exist.

The Introduction refers to several popular versions of architects as
heroes. This highly romanticized image of the architect in
American culture is both misleading and oversimplified. In reality,
most architects are decidedly unheroic, although many have idio-
syncratic personalities. Consider some of their mannerisms and
attitudes, their social and behavioral characteristics. As you read,
try to envision a particular architect, or even the architect you
yourself may become.

Architects as Types

Some people seem destined to be architects, possessing natural
talents as designers. Others are born into circumstances that
facilitate achieving personal and professional goals with minimal resistance. Notwithstanding their intellectual and artistic
talents, the latter are blessed at birth with social status, useful

personal contacts, and perhaps inherited wealth. They have a head start giving them access to a world of potential clients not readily available to others. Comfortable and confident, armed with charm and sophistication, they can practice architecture as an artistic and cultural pursuit rather than as a business or career. If the elite influence much of what is built, and someone has grown up among the elite, unfettered by subsistence finances, then being an elite architect can be a sure ticket to success.

Another type, the architectural artiste, is defined by manner, not social background or inherent talent and intellect. Through gestures and words, artistes typically express themselves flamboyantly and unconventionally. They can be witty, deadly serious, or dramatic, but they are never shy. They are demonstrative and relish an audience. Much of what artistes do is consciously chosen or fashioned to express their artistic tastes and to put on a show: what they wear, how they live, the authors they read and quote, the diversions they seek.

Common to all professions, but sometimes extreme in architecture, are the prima donna types. They can be oblivious to and even disdainful toward other people, ideas, and activities unconnected to their own interests and needs. They often seem arrogant, pompous, vain and temperamental. Prima donnas also may act the artiste, affecting defiant nonconformity. Some prima donnas, having made their mark, can legitimately claim the limelight. Others are less deserving, their self-estimation, not the estimation of others, placing them on a pedestal. Humility eludes most prima donna architects, who will not hesitate to tell you how accomplished they are.

Architecture always has creative fantasizers who dream up and propose projects that seem unrealizable. The fantasizer is not deterred by matters of practicality, convention, or acceptability. A speculator and risk taker in the realm of ideas, the fantasizer may also take pleasure in being outrageous and iconoclastic, using fantasy as a form of criticism or commentary. Stretching the boundaries of style, scale, or technology, design fantasies can be simultaneously satirical, vexatious, symbolic, and enlightening. Often fantasizers brew up fantasy for its own sake, to be whimsical and amusing. Only when pretending to be real or denying reality do their efforts deserve skepticism or dismissal, since confusing fantasy with reality can be dangerous.

By contrast, many architects are pragmatic, down-to-earth types. They are practical, get-the-job-done people who prefer reality to fantasy. They may seem anti-intellectual, but in fact they embrace intellectual concepts that make sense and prove useful. They like

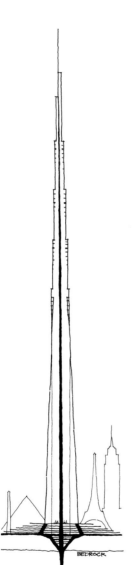

Frank Lloyd Wright's fantasy, the mile-high "Illinois" tower for Chicago, to contain 18,462,000 square feet of space and 130,000 occupants.

building for its own sake and thrive on the nitty-gritty process of design and construction, happily worrying about costs and deadlines. Down-to-earth architects, eschewing aesthetic speculation and verbal theorizing, are less concerned about the meaning of beauty than in finding the means to achieve beauty.

Practical architects also may have strong management and organizational skills, reflecting their interest in project implementation. We speak of architects who know how to put buildings together—who are knowledgeable about detailed design, construction materials and systems, and construction procedures. But preoccupation with practicality can impede innovative design thinking, since the most practical approach is to continue doing what was done before. Thus there is a strong argument for design teams composed of those who dream up ideas and those who can execute them.

Architects of any type can be compulsive, even obsessive, about their work. Being somewhat compulsive as an architect is not necessarily bad. Hundreds of tasks in architectural practice require intense, careful, thorough execution. God and the devil are in the details. Thus, being compulsive about pursuing and completing a task 100 percent is an asset in an architectural office where exhaustive, nitpicking, time-intensive work must be diligently and meticulously carried out. Public safety depends on such diligence. Wouldn't you feel more comfortable in a building whose design was scrutinized by a compulsive architect than by a hang-loose architect?

Being obsessive-compulsive is a liability when it becomes extreme and irrational. It leads to intellectual and emotional blindness, eclipsing potentially desirable options and possibilities. Excessively compulsive architects alienate colleagues and clients by stubbornly rejecting intelligent compromises. Clinging unrelentingly to beloved geometric forms, styles, materials, or colors, no matter how inappropriate, architects sometimes build ghastly architecture driven only by personal obsession with their own bad ideas. Of course, do not confuse irrational obsession with reasoned tenacity and commitment. A fine line distinguishes vigorous advocacy from compulsive defensiveness, but it is an important distinction.

Architectural offices are full of plodders. Plodders, like down-to-earth and reasonably compulsive architects, are necessary in architectural practice. They willingly undertake work that requires steady, laborious, and often tedious effort. They just keep on going, plugging away until the job is done. They cope well with drudgery, of which there is much in architecture. The plodder is persistent but not necessarily obsessive. Faced with an obstacle or change of direction, he or she may adapt readily to changed circumstances. Most plodders generally respect authority and gladly accept instruction or guidance.

The business of architecture naturally engenders business types. Many architects choose to become, or evolve into, managers and entrepreneurs. Managers like to be in charge, exercise power, direct people, and conduct operations. They enjoy responsibility and authority. To be effective, they need leadership ability and the ability to make decisions in situations of conflict and pressure. Their instincts draw them to organizations and to organizational politics.

In architectural practice, both projects and firms require management. In this respect, architecture is like any other business. Firm accounts, finances, personnel, business development, equipment, and physical facilities have to be administered, along with specific, day-to-day project operations. Without strong management, organizational chaos and financial failure are likely. Thus professional managers are among the most critical and highly paid workers, even in architectural practice.

But managers can be a problem as well. Tinkering with administrative structures or interfering with firm operations, managers can stifle those working under them. The passive, laissez-faire manager can be just as obstructive by failing to provide adequate leadership and direction. He or she risks letting things slip out of control or slip through altogether. Although the casual manager may superficially maintain amiable relations with underlings, lack of attention and guidance may result in frustrated and demoralized personnel, and even mission failure. Good managers may not always be loved, but they will be respected, listened to, and usually rewarded, no matter how obnoxiously or pleasantly they may behave from time to time.

Not all managers are entrepreneurs. Entrepreneurs are, above all, risk takers willing to accept the possibility of loss as well as gain. Consciously or subconsciously, they may thrive on risk. Entrepreneurs like to create and control businesses or projects, to own them, not just manage them. Conscious of the marketplace, they are always alert to new opportunities, which they try to exploit. Anyone who enjoys generating ideas and then mustering resources to implement them is an entrepreneur. Entrepreneurs also have to do a lot of networking, which requires many of the social and verbal skills discussed in previous chapters. The best networkers are extroverts who join and participate in professional, civic, and social organizations, mixing with both colleagues and prospective clients. Meeting people, exchanging ideas, gathering information and project leads, and making themselves or their firms more widely known is how most architects conduct public relations.

Many architects aspire to be "Renaissance" persons. The Renaissance in Europe—stretching from the fifteenth to the seventeenth centuries—was the age of discovery, secular enlightenment, and humanism. It produced some of Western civilization's most creative inventors, artists, architects, philosophers, craftsmen, scientists, engineers, and builders: Leonardo da Vinci, Michelangelo, Andrea Palladio, and Isaac Newton, among others. Thus, when we characterize someone as a Renaissance person, we are recognizing his or her diverse talents, intelligence, skills, and versatility—someone who can be both a generalist and a specialist.

Such aspirations still make sense for architects. To be an architect today requires expertise in a variety of disciplines, coupled with the ability to respond effectively to an environment of increasing complexity, uncertainty, and change. Architects must be able to work intelligently with masons as well as bankers, with accountants as well as digital computers. They must be artists, poets, engineers, sociologists, business administrators, and diplomats. Trying to be a Renaissance person is challenging, but many architects come close to it. And although the prolific Renaissance architect of today may not produce cutting-edge or timeless architecture, he or she may very well be the type who has the best crack at it.

Idols and Adulation

Every period, movement, and trend in architecture has its architectural heroes and heroines—individuals widely recognized and celebrated within the profession. A few become public figures. They may be admired not only for their design work but also for their theories and teachings, their critical insights, or their artistic and literary skills. The culture of architecture seems unable to exist

Frank Lloyd Wright in his studio.

without a pantheon-du-jour, a collection of designated prophets and apostles blessed for the moment by their peers, historians and critics, academics and students, and journalists. Membership in the pantheon changes regularly, but there is always a pantheon. And only a few members—like Frank Lloyd Wright, Le Corbusier, and Louis Kahn—are likely to remain permanent members.

Architectural prophets and apostles must stand for more than the Vitruvian ideal of "commodity, firmness, and delight." Today's culture does not worship mere competence, but rather idolizes the avant-garde whose work, appearing new and iconoclastic, is most visually provocative. Heroes may reveal in some way the transcendental essence of architecture, its poetic power. Some practitioner heroes have made their poetic revelations explicit by writing or telling us about them. Such discourses can be intellectually fascinating or, at worst, obscure and pedantic. Sometimes they bear little relationship to the tangible architecture at hand.

Architecture is rich in messages. Too often, though, we hear pronouncements of meaning and symbolism that only the heroic architect, acting as the messenger, along with a select group of sympathetic critics and disciples, can see or interpret. Such interpretations may elude the rest of us no matter how hard we try to make sense of them. Consequently be wary of what you hear and read about idolized heroes. Maintain an open but critical mind. Architecture is full of overworked, tiresome, inappropriately used design clichés that are the residue of some heroic designer's once original ideas. And many so-called original design ideas, touted by journalists in search of the hottest story, may, in fact, be bad ideas.

The Faces of an Evolving Profession

In my architecture class at MIT in the 1960s, there was one woman; the rest of us were white, American-born males, mostly young and single. Today the demographics have changed dramatically. Women make up close to half the population of architecture students in North America. White males of European descent still dominate, but today's architecture school classes are composed of many more students of Asian, Hispanic and African descent. Most are Americans, but a good number are foreign students from countries around the world—China, Korea, Japan, Thailand, India, Iran, Turkey, Israel, Egypt, South Africa, Brazil, Argentina—not to mention Europe and Australia.

Architecture students are not only ethnically and nationally diverse, they also are more diverse in age and social background. Increasing numbers study at the graduate level, have degrees and experience in other fields, and are heads of households. No longer is it unusual to see middle-aged men or women studying alongside twenty-year-olds in architecture school.

But some things still have not changed as much or as rapidly as one might hope or expect. White males still dominate the profession. Most architectural firm owners, senior officials of the AIA, and professors in architecture schools are white males. African Americans are relatively sparse in the architecture profession and on architecture faculties, as well as in architecture school student bodies, despite decades of affirmative action on the part of universities. There are several explanations.

Women clearly face pressures that men do not. During child-bearing and child-rearing years, many women architects are unable to devote their full attention and energies to professional activities, thereby falling behind their male counterparts in seniority and experience. Until the 1980s, female architects as a group were still considerably younger statistically than male architects and therefore were less likely to have attained leadership positions in practice or teaching. However, women are increasingly taking their place in the profession alongside men.

African Americans in high school and college have tended to choose careers other than architecture, perhaps continuing to perceive architecture as a "white male" profession. Statistically there are still relatively few African American architect mentors or role models. Yet in the United States, black architects have a long and successful history in both private practice and government, and African American graduate architects find jobs as readily as anyone else. Within African American families and communities, architecture still seems to be an especially remote and esoteric profession, one rarely considered by students who nevertheless might have the requisite talents and motivation. Even predominantly black colleges have to work hard persuading students to go into architecture.

Ideally the ethnicity, sex, and national origin of an architect should be irrelevant, since individual's abilities, dedication, and unique personality are what matter most in architecture. Therefore, no matter who you are or where you come from or what you look like, if you want to be an architect and have the talent, nothing stands in your way.

Afterword

I feel compelled to offer a few, brief reminders and parting observations, plus my thanks to you for reading this book.

On Becoming an Architect

- After high school spend at least two years, if not more, pursuing college-level general education before concentrating on architecture in a professional program. Play the field of electives, explore diverse interests, engage in sports, travel a bit, and find yourself prior to three or four years of total architectural immersion. It is difficult to get all this in when you go directly from high school into a five-year, undergraduate B.Arch. program.

- In selecting architectural schools, be skeptical of architectural school rankings published annually, in particular the *U.S. News and World Report* college and university survey (typically appearing in March). It identifies its top twenty architecture schools by sending questionnaires only to deans and one or two senior faculty of schools granting master's degrees, asking them to "rank the reputations of schools" based on "scholarship, curriculum, and the quality of faculty and graduate students." The response rate is about 50 to 60 percent. This ranking methodology is superficial and seriously flawed. It ignores the views of most architecture faculty as well as practicing architects and school alumni; it overlooks B.Arch. programs; it assumes current deans and senior faculty are the most knowledgeable about other schools' curriculum, courses, and faculty, a dubious assumption; and, with its focus on reputation, it inevitably pushes image over substance. It should come as no surprise that the alma maters of deans and senior faculty repeatedly dominate the list.

- If you are studying architecture but doing poorly or feeling unhappy about it, consider alternatives: taking a year off to work, enrolling in fewer courses, or even changing majors. Architecture is not easy, but it should be stimulating, satisfying, and even fun.

- You may want to look for schools offering optional academic tracks for students after completion of introductory architectural studies. These tracks would be alternatives to the traditional track emphasizing and centered on design. Such programs serve well the many architectural students who discover that architectural design is not their strength but who have strengths in other areas—history and theory, urban planning, technology, landscape architecture, interior and furniture design, and management, for example.

• Architectural schools should educate fewer but better architects. At the same time they should seek more institutional support for expanding nonprofessional components of their programs, allowing them to offer more courses for undergraduates and others not intending to seek professional architectural degrees but who are interested in the subject. Nevertheless, the accredited professional program should not be compromised for the sake of nonprofessional, general education.

On Being an Architect

• If and when you marry, consider its impact on your career and your career's impact on your marriage. Marrying and having children at too young an age can be stressful for architects who work long hours for moderate compensation. And there is a lot to be said for marrying someone who is *not* an architect—ideally someone capable of earning a living independently. Even better, marry someone with money.

• Take your time. There is no rush. You do not have to do it all before you are thirty or even forty. You have much to learn, and architects are students all their lives, capable of learning new things and starting in new directions at any age.

• Be assured that today's fads and fashions will be stale tomorrow and gone by next week. What seems important now may be inconsequential in the future. Architects must search for more lasting values, just as their buildings must endure for decades or centuries. Even architectural journalists, critics, and teachers are not immune to judging architecture too much by the standards of the moment.

• Resist the temptation to be all things to all people. Genuine architects do best when they are doing architecture. They are dif-

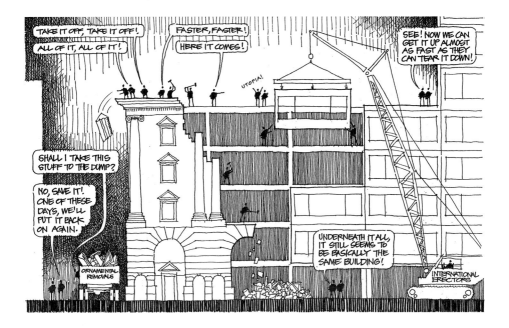

ferent from engineers, contractors, sociologists, financial analysts, or developers. Therefore, concentrate on improving the circumstances that relate directly to architecture and architectural practice, avoiding periodic forays into other territory just for the sake of economic expedience. Creating good architecture and good cities is a great enough challenge.

• Recall what makes architecture such an appealing profession to so many: the excitement and rewards of design and building; the process of creating useful and visually rich environments; the fusion of art, technology, and the social sciences in one discipline; the opportunity to exercise community leadership; and the occasional gratitude and recognition bestowed by respectful clients, colleagues, and the public. The impediments, frustrations, financial limitations, and risks that architects must cope with make it an undeniably challenging career. For those with talent, motivation, and some amount of good luck, no career is quite like architecture.

Appendix: Accredited Programs in Architecture

The Association of Collegiate Schools of Architecture (ACSA), 1735 New York Avenue, N.W., Washington, D.C., 20006, offers a number of publications for prospective architecture students. They include: *Guide to Architecture Schools,* a comprehensive catalog of schools; *ACSA Annual Directory,* a list of architecture school addresses, phone and fax numbers, and faculty data; and *Architecture Schools: Special Programs,* about summer, introductory, and foreign studies programs. Contact schools individually to obtain specific information about programs, degrees, costs, financial aid, faculty, and admissions requirements. Following is a list of both B.Arch and M.Arch programs accredited by the National Architectural Accrediting Board as of 1997.

Andrews University, Department of Architecture
Berrien Springs, Michigan 49104-0450
(616) 471-3309

Arizona, University of, College of Architecture
Tucson, Arizona 85721
(602) 621-6751

Arizona State University, College of Architecture
Tempe, Arizona 85287-1605
(602) 965-3536

Arkansas, University of, School of Architecture
Fayetteville, Arkansas 72701
(501) 575-4945

Auburn University, College of Architecture, Design and Construction
Auburn, Alabama 36849-5313
(334) 844-4524

Ball State University, College of Architecture and Planning
Muncie, Indiana 47306
(317) 285-5861

Boston Architectural Center
Boston, Massachusetts 02115
(617) 536-3170

California at Berkeley, University of, Department of Architecture
Berkeley, California 94720
(415) 642-4942

California at Los Angeles, University of, Department of Architecture
and Urban Design
Los Angeles, California 90095-1467
(310) 825-0525

California College of Arts and Crafts, School of Architectural Studies
San Francisco, California 94103
(415) 703-9561

California Polytechnic State University, Architecture Department
San Luis Obispo, California 93407
(805) 546-1316

California State Polytechnic University, Pomona, Department of Architecture
Pomona, California 91768-4048
(909) 869-2682

Carnegie-Mellon University, Department of Architecture
Pittsburgh, Pennsylvania 15213-3890
(412) 268-2355

Catholic University of America, School of Architecture and Planning
Washington, D.C. 20064
(202) 319-5188

Cincinnati, University of, School of Architecture and Interior Design
Cincinnati, Ohio 45221-0016
(513) 556-6426

City College of the City University of New York, School of Architecture
and Environmental Studies
New York, New York 10031
(212) 650-7118

Clemson University, College of Architecture
Clemson, South Carolina 29634-0501
(864) 656-3085

Colorado, University of, at Denver College of Architecture and Planning
Denver, Colorado 80217-3364
(303) 556-3382

Columbia University, Graduate School of Architecture, Planning and
Preservation
New York, New York 10027
(212) 854-3510

Cooper Union, Irwin S. Chanin School of Architecture
New York, New York 10003-7183
(212) 353-4220

Cornell University, Department of Architecture
Ithaca, New York 14853-6701
(607) 255-5236

Detroit Mercy, University of, School of Architecture
Detroit, Michigan 48219-0900
(313) 993-1532

Drexel University, Department of Architecture
Philadelphia, Pennsylvania 19104
(215) 895-2409

Drury College, Hammons School of Architecture
Springfield, Missouri 65802
(417) 873-7288

Florida, University of, Department of Architecture
Gainesville, Florida 32611-5702
(352) 392-0205

Florida A&M University, School of Architecture
Tallahassee, Florida 32307
(904) 599-3244

Frank Lloyd Wright School of Architecture
Scottsdale, Arizona 85261-4430
(602) 860-2700

Georgia Institute of Technology, College of Architecture
Atlanta, Georgia 30332-0155
(404) 894-3881

Hampton University, Department of Architecture
Hampton, Virginia 23668
(804) 727-5440

Harvard University, Department of Architecture
Cambridge, Massachusetts 02138
(617) 495-2591

Hawaii, University of, at Manoa, School of Architecture
Honolulu, Hawaii 96822
(808) 956-7225

Houston, University of, College of Architecture
Houston, Texas 77204-4431
(713) 743-2400

Howard University, School of Architecture and Planning
Washington, D.C. 20059
(202) 806-7420

Idaho, University of, Department of Architecture
Moscow, Idaho 83844-2451
(208) 885-6781

Illinois Institute of Technology, College of Architecture
Chicago, Illinois 60616
(312) 567-3260

Illinois, University of, at Chicago, School of Architecture
Chicago, Illinois 60607-7024
(312) 996-3335

Illinois, University of, at Urbana-Champaign, School of Architecture
Champaign, Illinois 61820
(217) 333-1330

Iowa State University, Department of Architecture
Ames, Iowa 50011-3093
(515) 294-4717

Kansas, University of, School of Architecture and Urban Design
Lawrence, Kansas 66045
(913) 864-4281

Kansas State University, College of Architecture, Planning and Design
Manhattan, Kansas 66506-2901
(913) 532-5953

Kent State University, School of Architecture and Environmental Design
Kent, Ohio 44242
(330) 672-2917

Kentucky, University of, College of Architecture
Lexington, Kentucky 40506-0041
(606) 257-7617

Lawrence Technological University, College of Architecture & Design
Southfield, Michigan 48075
(810) 204-2805

Louisiana State University, College of Design
Baton Rouge, Louisiana 70803
(504) 388-5400

Louisiana Tech University, School of Architecture
Ruston, Louisiana 71272
(318) 257-2816

Maryland, University of, at College Park, School of Architecture
College Park, Maryland 20742-1411
(301) 405-6284

Massachusetts Institute of Technology, Department of Architecture
Cambridge, Massachusetts 02139
(617) 253-7791

Miami, University of, School of Architecture
Coral Gables, Florida 33124
(305) 284-5000

Miami University, Department of Architecture
Oxford, Ohio 45056
(513) 529-1964

Michigan, University of, College of Architecture and Urban Planning
Ann Arbor, Michigan 48109-2069
(313) 764-1300

Minnesota, University of, Department of Architecture
Minneapolis, Minnesota 55455
(612) 624-7866

Mississippi State University, School of Architecture
Mississippi State, Mississippi 39762
(601) 325-2202

Montana State University, School of Architecture
Bozeman, Montana 59717
(406) 994-4255

Morgan State University, Institute of Architecture and Planning
Baltimore, Maryland 21239
(410) 319-3225

Nebraska-Lincoln, University of, College of Architecture
Lincoln, Nebraska 68588-0106
(402) 472-3592

New Jersey Institute of Technology, School of Architecture
Newark, New Jersey 07102
(201) 596-3079

New Mexico, University of, School of Architecture and Planning
Albuquerque, New Mexico 87131
(505) 277-2903

New York Institute of Technology, School of Architecture and Design
Old Westbury, New York 11568
(516) 686-7593

North Carolina, University of, at Charlotte, College of Architecture
Charlotte, North Carolina 28223
(704) 547-2358

North Carolina State University, Department of Architecture
Raleigh, North Carolina 27695-7701
(919) 515-8350

North Dakota State University, Department of Architecture & Landscape
Architecture
Fargo, North Dakota 58105
(701) 231-8614

Norwich University, Division of Architecture and Art
Northfield, Vermont 05663
(802) 485-2620

Notre Dame, University of, School of Architecture
Notre Dame, Indiana 46556
(219) 631-6137

Ohio State University, Austin E. Knowlton School of Architecture
Columbus, Ohio 43210
(614) 292-5567

Oklahoma, University of, Division of Architecture
Norman, Oklahoma 73019-0265
(405) 325-2444

Oklahoma State University, School of Architecture
Stillwater, Oklahoma 74078-0185
(405) 744-6043

Oregon, University of, Department of Architecture
Eugene, Oregon 97403
(541) 346-3656

Parsons School of Design Department of Architecture and
Environmental Design
New York, New York 10011
(212) 229-8955

Pennsylvania, University of, Department of Architecture
Philadelphia, Pennsylvania 19104-6311
(215) 898-5728

Pennsylvania State University, College of Arts and Architecture
University Park, Pennsylvania 16802-1425
(814) 865-9535

Prairie View A&M University, Department of Architecture
Prairie View, Texas 77446-0397
(409) 857-2014

Pratt Institute, School of Architecture
Brooklyn, New York 11205
(718) 399-4308

Princeton University, School of Architecture
Princeton, New Jersey 08544
(609) 258-3741

Puerto Rico, University of, School of Architecture
San Juan, Puerto Rico 00931-1909
(809) 250-8581

Rensselaer Polytechnic Institute, School of Architecture
Troy, New York 12180-3590
(518) 276-6460

Rhode Island School of Design, Department of Architecture
Providence, Rhode Island 02903
(401) 454-6280

Rice University, School of Architecture
Houston, Texas 77251-1892
(713) 527-4044

Roger Williams University, School of Architecture
Bristol, Rhode Island 02809
(401) 254-3605

Savannah College of Art and Design, Department of Architecture
Savannah, Georgia 31401
(912) 238-2487

South Florida, University of, School of Architecture and Community
Design
Tampa, Florida 33612-9421
(813) 974-4031

Southern California, University of, School of Architecture
Los Angeles, California 90089-0291
(213) 740-2723

Southern California Institute of Architecture
Los Angeles, California 90066
(310) 574-1123

Southern College of Technology, School of Architecture
Marietta, Georgia 30060-2896
(770) 528-7253

Southern University and A&M College, School of Architecture
Baton Rouge, Louisiana 70813
(504) 771-3015

Southwestern Louisiana, University of, School of Architecture
Lafayette, Louisiana 70504-3850
(318) 482-6225

State University of New York at Buffalo, School of Architecture and
Environmental Design
Buffalo, New York 14214-3087
(716) 829-3483

Syracuse University, School of Architecture
Syracuse, New York 13244-1250
(315) 443-2256

Temple University, Architecture Program
Philadelphia, Pennsylvania 19122
(215) 204-8813

Tennessee, University of, College of Architecture and Planning
Knoxville, Tennessee 37996-2400
(423) 974-5265

Texas, University of, at Arlington, School of Architecture
Arlington, Texas 76019
(817) 272-2801

Texas, University of, at Austin, School of Architecture
Austin, Texas 78712
(512) 471-1922

Texas A&M University, Department of Architecture
College Station, Texas 77843-3137
(409) 845-0129

Texas Tech University, College of Architecture
Lubbock, Texas 79409-2091
(806) 742-3136

Tulane University, School of Architecture
New Orleans, Louisiana 70118-5671
(504) 865-5389

Tuskegee Institute, Department of Architecture
Tuskegee Institute, Alabama 36088
(334) 727-8329

Utah, University of, Graduate School of Architecture
Salt Lake City, Utah 84112
(801) 581-8254

Virginia, University of, School of Architecture
Charlottesville, Virginia 22903
(804) 924-3715

Virginia Polytechnic Institute and State University, College of
Architecture and Urban Studies
Blacksburg, Virginia 24061-0205
(540) 231-6416

Washington, University of, Department of Architecture
Seattle, Washington 98195-5720
(206) 543-4180

Washington State University, School of Architecture
Pullman, Washington 99164-2220
(509) 335-5539

Washington University, School of Architecture
St. Louis, Missouri 63130
(314) 935-6200

Wentworth Institute of Technology, Department of Architecture
Boston, Massachusetts 02115-5998
(617) 442-9010

Wisconsin-Milwaukee, University of, Department of Architecture
Milwaukee, Wisconsin 53201
(414) 229-5564

Woodbury University, Department of Architecture
Burbank, California 91510-7846
(818) 767-0888

Yale University, School of Architecture
New Haven, Connecticut 06520
(203) 432-2288

At this writing, five candidacy programs have applications pending for
NAAB accreditation: University of the District of Columbia; University of
Nevada, Las Vegas; New School of Architecture, San Diego; Philadelphia
College of Textiles and Science; Polytechnic University of Puerto Rico;
and Polytechnic University of Puerto Rico.